WHO
IS
ZORA?

SIGHT UNSEEN

"Dis" the "Dis" in Disability

ZORA MESSING NATANBLUT

WHO
IS
ZORA?
SIGHT UNSEEN
"Dis" the "Dis" in Disability

Capucia
PUBLISHING

Published by:
Capucia, LLC
211 Pauline Drive #513
York, PA 17402
www.capuciapublishing.com

ISBN: 978-1-945252-81-5
Library of Congress Control Number: 2020911724

Cover Design: Ranilo Cabo
Layout: Ranilo Cabo
Editor and Proofreader: Jennifer Crosswhite
Book Midwife: Carrie Jareed

Printed in the United States of America

Dedication

With love to my teenage sweetheart, Herman.
He is still holding my hand
as we are walking through our golden years.

Zora & Herman at camp / wedding / 25th & 50th anniversaries /
children: Amy, Leah, Adam.

Your beliefs become your thoughts.

Your thoughts become your words.

Your words become your actions.

Your actions become your habits.

Your habits become your values.

Your values become your destiny.

Mahatma Gandhi

Contents

I Welcome Possibilities into My Life!

I never imagined myself ever writing this book. In fact, I never envisioned myself writing ANY book. Especially a book about the very thing that has caused me great suffering and pain. But here we are. I wrote it, and it's a joy to share it with you now.

For most of my life, I had been living what could best be described as an **un**authentic life. Instead of dealing with the limitation I was born with, I have studiously followed the path laid down for me by well-meaning adults. Be a good, quiet, kind little girl, and never ever mention your disability. Your appearance and agility make you appear "normal." I became an actress playing the role of me.

At some level, I knew the challenges that I entered this life with were intended to teach me the things that I needed to know in order to grow. I have accepted the lessons that I have learned, even though I may not understand on strictly a cognitive level why I made particular choices. I have worked hard to commit to learning, growing, and living authentically.

As a child, I conformed in thought and behavior to the story about me created by my family, my teachers, my doctors, and my classmates. I looked and acted age appropriate. At an early age, I picked up my cues from listening and reading the body language of those around me. However, at school, in the classroom, or gym, these stories made me feel labeled: DISABLED, LESS THAN, NOT GOOD ENOUGH, STUPID, SLOW, INCOMPETENT, CLUMSY, and DIFFERENT.

All my life I struggled with the issue of vision, both seeing and being seen. For some inexplicable reason, I was born with a major defect. This is a condition of my life—not a medical issue. It is a fact that cannot be changed by an operation, medicine, or other interventions. There was no previous family history nor do my children or grandchildren have this problem.

As a result of my situation, I have endured many challenges, rejections, and disappointments. At times, these have made me feel regret, anger, and resentment. Looking at the past this way wastes my energy. I have discovered that dwelling on these misfortunes doesn't help. I am *not* "my story!" Suffering is optional. And I opt to no longer do this.

How and when did I find the strength to let go of the things that I could not change? The answer to that pivotal question is what this book will explore. It is also my hope to share the lessons I have learned along the way. I want to remove the abstractness of the old adage "with age comes wisdom" and provide concrete evidence of what I have actually learned.

Some of my most salient insights include the importance of being my own best friend as well as a good friend to others. For people to believe in me, I must believe in myself and recognize and accept that I am a work in progress. Also my parents encouraged me to do sports because they enjoyed them. They never said that ice or roller skating, skiing, and riding a two-wheeler could be dangerous. As a child, the only restriction I had was not crossing a street by myself.

Today, I acknowledge my entire God-given gifts and use them for *tikkun olam* (to make the world a better place). I believe that my life's purpose is to live authentically; thus I need to accept my abilities and limitations. I am a Conservative Jew who keeps a kosher home and observes the holidays. Herman, my husband, and I are founding members of our synagogue, Or Shalom, in Pennsylvania.

My mission is to help others to see their own beauty and self-worth so that they, too, will be an example for others. I am working diligently daily to give up my persona, my story, to be the person I am capable of being—a person who believes in herself and who can finally speak up for herself. I am becoming the mistress of my mind. I now trust my gut feelings. I let them guide me. This has been a long journey, but isn't that what life is all about? Now I want to bask in it and give to you, dear reader, what I have found for myself: self-acceptance. I now can expose what I was brought up to never, ever talk about: my life's secret—I was born legally blind!

My hope is you will join me on this journey to wholeness through self-acceptance. This road, at times, has felt like a roller coaster ride with happy highs and depressing lows; but it helped me to make peace with the past while living in the present. Gradually, I have been able to relinquish old, outdated stories so that I could expand my perspective.

I have found repeating affirmations extremely helpful; so I begin each chapter with an affirmation. With today's social media, secrets seem to be a thing of the past. We now live in a show-and-tell-all world. My last chapter, Dis the Dis in Disability, tells the story of many famous people who didn't let a disability hold them back from fame and fortune.

I hope you find value in the following pages, especially the self-help action exercises at the end of each chapter.

A vision board can be thought of as a graphic made up of pictures and words. It is a cue card for the unconscious to take you in the direction you wish to go. It can help you manifest what you want even if you are not aware of what you want. It became a visual beginning for my writing this memoir.

Vision Board

Before I put a word on paper, I made a vision board of who I am. It then escalated into who I wished to become.

It is easy and fun to do. It is cost effective. No real skills are needed.

A Vision Board pictorial outline of "Who is Zora?"

Action Exercise

Materials needed

- Bulletin board
- Scissors
- Glue, decorative tape, clear adhesive tape
- Old magazines, newspapers, greeting cards, picture postcards, photographs
- Glitter, ribbon, shells, buttons, textured material

Set up at a table with good lighting and background music you enjoy. Then go through the magazines, cutting out any pictures and/or words that call to you.

If in doubt, cut it out.

Sort cutouts into topics and store in labeled envelopes until ready to assemble.

Assemble and put it on display where you can view it frequently.

It might become a never-ending project, as there is always something else to add.

This becomes your pictorial outline.

Enjoy!

CHAPTER 1

Who Is Zora?

I approve of myself and love myself deeply and completely.

Mirror, Mirror
Mirror, Mirror you see deep
Beyond my dreams and into sleep,
Unlocking secrets that I keep.

Secrets that hold me back,
Listing things that I lack,
Puts me on the attack.

Dreams reveal myself to me,
The part I do not wish to see.
What will set me free?

Affirmations help me cope,
Give me a handle and some hope
To go beyond this slippery slope.

Who is that person in my dream
With that demeaning theme?
Is it Zora Sight Unseen?

Poem by Zora Messing Natanblut

The idea of writing a book came to me nearly two decades ago when I was playing on the floor with both my infant and toddler grandchildren. That book would have been called, *When Grandma Zora Was a Little Girl*. However, as sometimes happens with plans, time managed to slip by more quickly than my pen and paper could get together to write that story. In what feels like the blink of an eye, my grandchildren have become teenagers and young adults. The focus of writing a book now has become more for me than them. Thus, it will be a personal memoir.

Writing this memoir feels like a birthing process. Pregnancy, like writing, seems to trigger varied emotions: humorous highs, sobbing lows, and tranquil, thought-filled moments. There are *aha* moments of great joy and elation. Then there are other moments of frustration when the words won't flow or the computer misbehaves. Writing rearranges my daily schedule, including my sleep time. This puts me on an emotional roller coaster of a different kind of extreme highs and lows. Time seems to slow down when I want it to speed up and vice versa.

Actually, mine has been a very fulfilling life while dealing with a major, invisible physical challenge. Not only was it invisible, but it was also a secret. So, I was totally unaware that I saw things differently than my peers. "Challenge" became the buzzword when approaching my sixty-fifth birthday. Sixty-five didn't feel old, but being able to collect Social Security made me believe that I had reached my geriatric years.

This milestone spurred greater introspection than usual. I asked myself tons of questions that all boiled down to the same thing. What personal accomplishments was I truly proud of? What else could I strive to complete?

It felt important to have a last hurrah to cast myself finally as *numero uno*. First listing things that I enjoyed doing and then challenging myself to excel at them. My friends were no longer interested in challenges or competitions. They were ready to retire and relax. My mind said, "This is your last time to go for the gold." You will read about my sixty-fifth birthday challenges and accomplishments later.

I survived that year valiantly and, as a result, changed my beliefs and self-image. I finally was able to acknowledge that I had the drive and the stamina to come in first. That year I was able to live by Eleanor Roosevelt's dictum, "Do something scary every day."

Now more than ten years later, I have a new goal. This memoir shows that I have transformed myself from the *poor me* person wallowing in the disappointment of having a physical handicap to an accomplished, competent, successful, and self-accepting adult.

The Past

When I was a small child, I always dreamed of being a mother, with more daughters than sons. There were dreams of being "Sweet Sixteen" and wearing a beautiful, flowing long dress to my birthday party and having a boyfriend who someday would be the father to my children. Our wedding would be a regal affair.

Zora and her parents at her Sweet Sixteen.

Of course at the time, I didn't realize that these dreams were probably the same as those of every other young girl of my era. My parents' enthusiasm and generosity helped me realize these fantasies. Career dreams were not part of my childhood aspirations.

Growing up Jewish in Brooklyn in the1940s and 1950s, girls didn't have much to aspire to other than being a homemaker. The respectable occupations for an educated woman who worked were either nurses or teachers. Girls might be praised for their domestic skills or their beauty. It was impolite for a girl to praise herself. If she did, she was thought to be conceited. "Give a girl too much praise and you will be spoiling her," was the psychology of the day.

The Present

I participated in a yoga class recently where the teacher was a couple of generations younger than her students. We students were in our 60s to late 80s. At the end of the class, the teacher asked us to hug ourselves. We did. It felt good. Then, as we were hugging ourselves, she asked us to say, "I am beautiful!" No one said a word. She repeated the statement, "Say, I am beautiful!" The silence grew more pervasive. After a third try, she moved on to another closing exercise. Obviously, our instructor was clueless as to why the class was unresponsive. We students were of the era where that was improper behavior.

In the locker room after yoga, we discussed how different our daughters' and granddaughters' upbringings have been from our own. We grandmothers all tended to lavish the praise on them which we rarely received as children. Our daughters and granddaughters are comfortable talking about their accomplishments. I still have difficulty doing that. As I have said elsewhere, that is one of my major motivations for writing this book: self-acknowledgment.

In the Beginning

I, Zora Estelle Isaacs, was born in a New York City hospital that no longer exists on March 27, 1940, on my maternal grandparents' thirty-sixth anniversary. That was an auspicious day. Eighteen and its multiples are special numbers in the Jewish religion. This comes from the fact that the Hebrew letters which form the word for *life* also represent the number eighteen. As a consequence, I grew up believing that of the five grandchildren, I was the favorite. Curiously, my three cousins also believed they were the favorite. My grandma Erna was a master at making each of us feels like we were the most loved and favorite grandchild, I hope and pray that I can make my grandchildren feel that way also.

I was a full-term, average-weight baby, the second child for my parents, three years younger than my brother, Robert. What wasn't obvious immediately about me was that I was born legally blind. This was discovered before my first birthday.

While feeding me in the kitchen, Louise, our cook and housekeeper, noticed that I only opened my mouth when the spoon touched my lips. My eyes didn't seem to follow the movement of the spoon.

Louise immediately brought this to my parents' attention. As a result, they took me to myriad eye specialists and pediatricians. Over the years, I was given an assortment of diagnoses: astigmatism, amblyopic, cone dystrophy, nearsighted in one eye and farsighted in the other eye. In essence, my eyes didn't work as a team. My parents were told that there wasn't anything that could be done for me because I was legally blind. So, they raised me as a normal child, never mentioning my visual disability to me or to anyone who didn't have a specific "need to know."

As a small child, I was overprotected and very well supervised so that I wouldn't get hurt. Until I went to school, I mainly played with my cousins and the children in my apartment building. None of these experiences made me feel like I had a vision or any other problem.

Before I started school, my mother talked to the principal and teachers about my vision. But nobody told me that my sight was different from that of most other children. Having never received any information to the contrary, I assumed that all children were like me. Starting with kindergarten, school was a cruel awakening.

Legally Blind
Legally blind is defined as having the visual acuity of 20/200 or less in the better eye using the best correction

possible. This means that a legally blind individual would have to stand 20 feet from an object to see it with the same degree of clarity as a normally sighted person could while standing 200 feet away. The top largest letter on an eye chart often represents visual acuity of 20/200.

Different cultures through history have depicted blindness in a variety of ways. The Greeks, for example, defined blindness as a punishment from the gods for which the afflicted individual was often granted compensation in the form of some other skill. Judeo-Christian literature expressed blindness as a flaw. It could be altered by contact with a holy man or relic. Almost without exception in early literature, blind people could bring this condition upon themselves through sin or trespasses against the gods.

As a child, I didn't know about these beliefs. In fact, it wasn't until I started writing this memoir that I learned about them. This is not part of my belief system. I have always believed in a benevolent God, not a vindictive one.

As an adult, I believe that I have lived many past lives. In most of them I had to deal with some form of physical disability. I also believe that each of us comes into this life with lessons to learn. This learning directs our life's path. I still have many miles to go on this path. I thought that if I could cope with my vision problem, then nothing else bad or terrible would happen to me. So far, I believe that contract continues.

Color Blind

I was born with cone dystrophy. It is the cones that differentiate colors in our vision. Women carry the gene for color blindness, but it is predominately men who have the condition. Approximately 1 in every 200 women are color blind compared to 1 in 12 men. Being color blind is something I don't usually talk about because it makes me feel less than whole or like a freak of nature.

Most men who are color blind don't seem to be at all ashamed or embarrassed about it. It is just a fact of life for them. Why then is it so hard for me to share this information about myself? It's not my fault that I was born this way. I know many of my friends and perhaps strangers who would be happy to help where color is involved. I just haven't been able to ask.

One of the indicators of maturing is being able to understand things through various lenses. Now that I'm in my later years, it's most curious to me that I can see the rational side of things as well as the nonrational. I can easily recognize how much easier my life would be if I could ask for assistance and matter of factly explain why I need the help. However, having lived so many decades obeying the admonition that family and personal issues need to remain a secret, it's been a near impossibility for me to reveal such information. Just putting this on paper is more than I thought I'd ever be able to do.

I'll let you in on another secret. After the last paragraph and throughout the rough draft of this memoir, many times I have added the following sentence in italics. *I might not keep this sentence/paragraph in the book.* Whatever it was that I wrote made me feel too exposed and vulnerable.

It's also possible that I feel a sense of pride in having created mechanisms for overcoming my limitations and, as a result, I would be offended by people offering to help me. It might diminish the independence I've been able to achieve.

Cone dystrophy is a general term used to describe a group of rare eye disorders that affect the cone cells of the retina. Cone dystrophy can cause a variety of symptoms including decreased visual clarity and sensitivity to light (photophobia). I have all these symptoms. Cone dystrophy may be broken down into two broad groups: stationary and progressive. In stationary cone dystrophy, which I have, symptoms tend to remain stable and are usually present at birth.

I now wonder how my mother, an amateur artist, felt having a color-blind daughter. Similarly, I try to imagine how Beverly Sills, the world-renowned opera singer, must have felt having had a daughter who was deaf. It's my belief that to know color is an intellectual process; to experience color is an emotional event. I imagine it is the same with music.

Mom and I never discussed my color blindness or any of my other visual problems. The adult me wants to know why. Did she carry some unnecessary mother's guilt? Did she just assume I would know that I had a vision problem? Would it have helped me if I knew I had limited vision and that I didn't see as well as my classmates? There are so many unanswered questions.

As a child, you are aware of only your own point of view and follow the lead of those closest to you. Since my mother never indicated that I had any visual shortcomings, it certainly never occurred to me that I did. My mother did what she could to make it less of a problem by color coordinating my wardrobe. She also would describe the color of the sunsets or shades and colors of flowers and trees in the park to me. So intellectually I understood the concept of color.

As an adult, the basics of my wardrobe are black and white. Any color can be used as an accent, even if I don't know what color I am choosing. Now that animal patterns are all the rage, my closet is full of zebra tops and bottoms. Recognizing that zebra stripes are always unique and only match if they are bought as a set, I select a solid color for a blouse to go with zebra pants and solid pants with a zebra top.

Last Names

You just read that the name on my birth certificate was Zora Estelle Isaacs. Upon entering school my name became Zora Estelle Messing. How can that be, you ask? My brother's and my last name were legally changed from Isaacs to Messing before I entered school. My maternal grandfather and his brothers only had daughters. There was no heir to carry on the Messing family name. My brother Robert was the first Messing grandchild. My mother the eldest daughter, always wanted to please her father and be recognized by him. Robert would carry on the family name and be the heir to Messing Bakery.

Because of my young age, the name change had no emotional effect on me. Also, as a female child, hopefully I would be changing my last name when I got married.

I felt this name change became a heavy psychological burden for my brother. He was already in elementary school and was aware of his last name change.

I have heard the story that when my father's parents came to the United States prior to World War I, their last name was changed to Isaacs. The immigration officers had a list of Jewish and biblical names to use if the presented name was not understood.

My father was a kind, caring, somewhat Victorian gentleman as far as his outlook on life. He was twelve years older than my mother. He and my maternal grandfather had a wonderful relationship. They enjoyed each other's company and spent time together. My father was Grandpa's unofficial financial and stock advisor. My father was generous and helped support his elderly, widowed mother and one of his sisters. Because of this, he was willing to allow his children to have his father-in-law's last name.

School

I remember very little of my life until I started kindergarten. I do remember having felt well-loved and cared for by my family at home.

Kindergarten was where I learned to be possessive of my belongings. I remember a boy sitting next to me taking some of my colored paper cut-out shapes or puzzle pieces. We used an assortment of straight lines, curves, and angles to form letters of the alphabet.

I didn't know how to speak up for myself and say my paper shapes were missing. I couldn't tell what specific colors were missing or tattle that the little boy next to me took them. In my life at home, there had always been an adult to see that things were in order. In school, I was on my own.

That became a big lesson! Hold on to your things and keep them in close range. Never let anyone else use them. Things may not get returned. "Neither a borrower nor a lender be," a quote from Shakespeare's *Hamlet* became my motto. I know that I am still that way today. I might happily give something of mine to you to keep if you ask to borrow it, but I will not lend it to you.

To this day, I remember the name of that little boy in kindergarten. I remember the feeling in the pit of my stomach because I couldn't describe the missing shapes by color. Being silent and upset seemed to be my only option. At school there was no adult to help me out.

So on one of the first few days of kindergarten, I learned how to disappear within myself. There no one could hurt me. I sat very still like the game of statues.

My breathing slowed, and I stared into space, making sure I was facing the teacher or blackboard. I could hear everything that was happening. I then moved into my internal fantasy world.

It was this same little boy who dipped the end of my long braids in the inkwell as he sat directly behind me in third grade. Needless to say, black ink splattered the back of my clothes and ruined them. In sixth grade, he invited me to the end of the year school dance. I guess he liked me. Funny how I was never able to let him know that his way of showing affection was quite misguided.

Art Class

As an elementary school student, art was all about pictures made with crayons or paint. I never used more than two colors at a time, one light and one dark. I preferred crayons to paint because crayons were labeled as to their color. Anything to do with art in school frightened me because I didn't see what everyone else saw. I believed art was all about seeing colors and their varying shades. I didn't want to expose myself. If I couldn't interpret colors, I shouldn't do art. But on the other hand, there was no way of avoiding art in school.

I live in a black-and-white world. My world is shades of light, medium, and dark. Unknowingly, the art teacher embarrassed me in front of my classmates in the seventh grade. Even today as I write this, I can see the classroom in my mind and feel the tall, thin female teacher staring at me. The class was learning about primary and secondary colors. It was a new lesson, so I hadn't memorized the color combinations.

The teacher asked me, "Zora, when mixed, what color does yellow and blue make?" I didn't answer. I froze and stared at the floor. My body became rigid, and I involuntarily held my breath. If I could have, I would have evaporated into the air or disappeared under the floor.

After repeating the question a second time, the teacher then pointed to a fluffy, satin hair ribbon around a ponytail of another student and asked, "Zora, what color is that ribbon Linda has in her hair? I sat there and continued to just stare at the ribbon. Someone else in the class finally answered, "Green." The teacher asked me to stay after class. I was humiliated in front of my friends. This gave my classmates something else to tease me about.

Even before the room was empty, the teacher began showing me colors and asking me to name them. Then she showed me two light colors and asked me if they were the same color? I felt attacked and helpless! I sat mute, embarrassed, ashamed, humiliated, and frightened. I tightly held my breath and tears. My stomach was churning inside me. The teacher made me feel like a lab rat being experimented on.

That day's activity was to paint a color wheel of primary and secondary colors. Mine remained blank. The teacher asked me to take the blank chart home and do it for homework. As soon as the teacher let me leave, I ran to the bathroom where I threw up and cried.

I gave the blank color wheel form to my mother and had her fill it in with watercolors. I know that my mother spoke to the teacher the very next day. I dreaded art class after that. I was terrified of the teacher. Fortunately, art was only once a week and only a semester long. The next semester I took shop, where I made an electric lamp in the shape of an old-fashioned water pump. I thoroughly enjoyed working with tools: sawing, sanding, staining, and electrifying it. The finished product looked good and was functional.

I was always dressed in the latest fashion, and everything I wore was color coordinated, thanks to my mother. I was brought up not to talk about my visual problems. This was not a medical problem, because no medicine or operation could fix it. This was just a fact of life that would follow me wherever I went for the rest of my life.

This young, uncoordinated, shy, well-behaved girl with poor eyesight is now a mature grown woman in the throes of retirement. She is still legally blind and color blind. Despite her poor sight, she has jumped through many hurdles. She is shy about praising or talking about her accomplishments, so she is writing this memoir. She also learned that there were many forms of art where color would not be a problem. Thus, she became involved with crafts. Crafts proved to be a fun and profitable hobby.

Ophthalmologists

As an adult, I find it amusing that as a color-blind person, my eye doctors' names were colors.

Dr. Brown, whose name is just about the only thing I remember about him, I saw from the time I was an infant until I started school. Dr. White I remember because I saw him yearly through my school years. He was tall, thin, with white hair and very pale, white skin. To me, he looked like a skinny Santa Claus with thin, wired, round glasses. He seemed very old and fragile.

His office was in a tall, brick building in New York City. Mom and I took the subway to the city, switching from the BMT (Brooklyn-Manhattan Transit) to the IRT (Independent Rapid Transit) train. I remember because in kindergarten I learned the alphabet. These letters were large on the train's window, and I could read them as the train stopped at the station in front of me. These were probably the first signs I was able to read.

Dr. White's office seemed very stuffy with heavy furniture and thick, dark Persian carpets. The room was always poorly lit. I think he might have done that for my benefit because I am photophobic. I remember he had a soft, gravelly voice. He was kind and gentle in his manner. He never talked down to me, even though I was a young child.

I always flinched when he shined a bright light into my eyes. I also hated when he handed me what looked like binoculars or opera glasses. When I put them up to my eyes, the left lens had a picture of a bird and the right lens had a picture of a birdcage. My task was to move the lens so that the bird was in the cage. Each of my eyes saw a different image, either a bird or a cage. I never could put the bird in the cage because my eyes didn't converge and work together. They still don't. I don't think ophthalmologists use this tool anymore or maybe just not with adults. I'm very grateful that I don't have to deal with this anymore. That exercise always frustrated me. I always believed that the next time I looked into the binoculars the bird would fly into the cage.

When I was in the first grade, my ophthalmology appointment with Dr. White was in the middle of a school day after lunch. My mom was going to pick me up at school during the class's rest hour. The class went up to the assembly room for nap time. There the pews had cushioned seats. Each child had his or her own personal little blanket and pillow.

I was left alone at my desk in our unlit classroom. I was scared; I am not sure of what. I had never been left totally alone, anywhere. My body started to shake. So, I took out my Palmer method writing workbook and my pencil. I scribbled away page after page until my mom arrived. Was I relieved to see her and hug her! She had to hold me in a tight hug to quiet my nervous system, which was still shaking.

I thought that I had done a great job writing in my workbook. I was certain my teacher would be so proud of me for not wasting time. But, the next day the teacher was not happy with me and erased all my work. I felt confused, ashamed, and disliked. I didn't know why. I was frustrated, angry, and upset because the teacher totally misread my intention. Why had she left me in the dark classroom all by myself? Didn't she know how frightening that was for me? The teacher never told me why she was erasing all my good work or why she was upset with me. I just decided that she didn't like me.

Incidents like this one made me want to run away and disappear. I pretended to be an invisible child. If I didn't look at the teacher, she wouldn't see me. Since I rarely spoke in class, she truly didn't hear me. Therefore, I believed I was invisible. If I wasn't there, I couldn't be hurt. I could just drift away into the clouds outside the window.

When my eye exam was over, I was sent outside the doctor's office to sit with the receptionist, a sweet older lady who looked like Mrs. Claus. This made me feel like I had done something wrong and the doctor was going to tell my mom about it. Why couldn't I stay and hear what the doctor was saying about me? Why did they make it a secret? If I had had a little knowledge or understanding that my vision was much less than everybody else's, maybe life at school would have been a little easier for me. Maybe then I could have asked for help when I needed it.

One only knows what one sees and hears, not what one doesn't see or hear!

Once the appointment was over, Mom and I would go to B. Altman's Department Store for lunch at the Bird Cage Restaurant. It got its name because the tables were surrounded by a simulated cage.

It was always a treat, like a ladies' lunch out, just me and Mom. Usually the time at home I spent with Mom was doing school work. That was never fun, just tedious. However, going to the restaurant made me feel so grown up. Though I could choose anything on the menu, I always ordered a tuna melt on white toast and a vanilla milkshake.

We usually did a little shopping before taking the subway back to our home in Brooklyn. I would pick the clothes that I liked, and Mom would color coordinate them into multiple mix-and-match outfits of skirts, blouses, and sweaters. Girls were not allowed to wear slacks to school no matter how cold it was outside. Tights were not in vogue yet.

In hindsight I now see the irony of eating at the Bird Cage. Mom and I were the birds in the cage! How easy it was to be the bird in the cage while eating. How frustrating for me to manipulate the binoculars and my eyes to put the bird in the cage. I wonder if my Mom ever thought about this irony. As a child I didn't know that I was a bird trapped in a cage, overprotected by the secret of my visual disability. Therefore, I had no idea that other children's vision was normal and mine was greatly limited.

Yes, I was a very sensitive child who did not know how to speak up for herself. I was not one to share my concerns, troubles, and thoughts, especially with authority figures like teachers. I am presently working on accepting the past. I am also working on living in the present where I can move into a healing and forgiving space as I write this memoir.

I find the words of the Dalai Lama helpful. "When I look at my own life...the suffering that I went through, each time I would have avoided it if I possibly could have. And yet when I look at the depth of my character now, isn't a part of that a product of those experiences? Weren't those experiences part of what created the depth of my inner being?"

How true I find his words. Growing up, certain topics were taboo to talk about outside the family: money, age, religion, politics, and problems. Being legally blind was my secret. I never mentioned it. If asked about my vision, I would say I have limited distance vision and then change the topic of conversation. Now as a mature adult, I am able to talk about it when someone asks me a question. But I will rarely initiate this conversation.

Once people hear those words "legally blind," there are two automatic responses. They either become overprotective and grab my arm to guide me. They forget that a minute earlier I was maneuvering very well on my own. They have even told me the things that they think are too dangerous for me to be doing like skiing, horseback riding, and bike riding. I have a few choice words I'd like to offer them. But, I hold my tongue. They think that they are being helpful and protective. Actually, I find their reaction demeaning and insulting.

Then there is the other reaction when people tell me how terrific they think I am because of all the things they see me do. They marvel at my abilities and accomplishments. Sometimes, they go on for too long, and I find that embarrassing. I have only recently learned to accept these as a compliment and just say, "Thank you."

My Dreams

Our ten-inch television in my parents' bedroom provided much of my home entertainment. I sat directly in front of the screen with my nose no more than ten inches away from the scene.

As a child watching TV, I envisioned myself riding the range with The Lone Ranger and Tonto or Roy Rogers and Gabby Hayes. As the heroine, I would be the one to put the bad guys in jail. I dreamed of wearing Dick Tracy's two-way radio wristwatch and solving all the mysteries. This watch was a dream back then. Look, it's a reality now in our electronic age.

It was TV's Molly Goldberg who would have fit most comfortably in my Jewish neighborhood. She could easily have been my Grandma Erna's friend and neighbor. They would have traded recipes. Each TV episode began with Molly calling to a neighbor out of her kitchen window. I can practically hear Mrs. Goldberg calling to me, "Yoo-hoo, Zora!"

While it was fun to fantasize about joining up with these TV characters, by the time I was a preteen, I began seeking some real-life heroines to emulate. Three famous women that I most admired were Maria Tallchief, a ballet dancer; Sonja Henie, an international champion ice skater; and Esther Williams, a world-renowned swimmer. Hollywood capitalized on Sonja and Esther's beauty and exceptional skills, transforming them into leading ladies of the cinema.

I admired their poise, skills, and agility as well as their regal posture and graceful movements. Each of these three women made it to the top of their profession. Perhaps the attraction for me stemmed from my own enjoyment of ice skating and swimming. When I was backstroking in the pool, I dreamed of being in a water ballet. As I did my jumps and spins on ice, I visualized and heard the crowd cheering for me. In reality, my experiences caused me to believe I was a totally uncoordinated klutz.

The Native American Maria Tallchief lived from the 1920s until the second decade of the twenty-first century. She began taking ballet lessons at three years old and became the first major prima ballerina of the New York City Ballet Company. She capitalized on her classic Native American beauty and height. Just three inches shy of six feet tall, she stood out from the other dancers. Her excellent balance, coordination, and rhythm were exemplary, and she kept perfect time with every musical note.

At the age of eight, I took ballet lessons in a dance studio at Ebbets Field. Even with "Dodger energy," I didn't become graceful. Ballet is much more difficult than it looks. A cute little tutu or costume didn't give me the grace, poise, or elegance I so desired. I quickly recognized that this was not the activity I would ever excel at.

Sonja Henie, born in Norway, debuted as an Olympic figure skater at the first Winter Games in 1924 at the age of eleven. Two years later, she won second place at the world figure skating championship, followed by three gold medals and ten consecutive world championships. After retiring from competitive skating, Henie became a movie star and toured around the world with her Hollywood Ice Skating Revue.

I knew about her mostly from her movies, which I watched on TV with my mom. Sonja Henie did for ice skating what Esther Williams did for swimming in the movies.

Ice Skating

There was a lovely public indoor skating rink not far from our home. The lake in Prospect Park would freeze over, and we could skate there. Skating on the lake could be tricky because of twigs, leaves, and bumps in the ice. No matter how cold and windy the day was, I never noticed it if I was skating.

Mom and I both enjoyed ice skating. As we would leave the house, skates slung over our shoulders, we would talk about our admiration for Sonja Henie and how we were going to emulate her movements on the ice. We usually skated Sunday afternoons at the indoor rink. I took some lessons and learned some simple jumps and spins. I loved feeling my long ponytail or braids fly out behind me when I would whip around the rink's corners. As my right leg crossed over my left, I crouched low like a racing skater cutting the corner sharply.

A number of my birthdays were celebrated at the ice rink. Halfway through the skating session there would be a break so that the ice could be resurfaced. That was when my friends and I would enjoy birthday cake and ice cream.

Some of my friends had never ice skated before. I was able to help them skate around the rink. Being able to help them didn't give me any particular feeling of pride or superiority. I knew even if I put the time in, I wasn't going far at this sport. Just like swimming, I enjoyed it enormously as a recreational activity but never held out any hope of excelling at it. I was not competitive and never saw myself as best at anything.

I also enjoyed roller skating. The roller skates clamped onto the front of my shoes. A metal skate key tightened the skate to the shoe. There was a leather strap that went around the ankle to hold my foot on the skate. The skates could elongate as my shoe size grew. The skates made a lovely clanging, scraping sound as I glided down the street. People could hear me coming and got out of my way. When I was skating fast, my arms were pumping at my sides. It almost felt like flying.

Buying new, white lace-up figure skates as my feet grew was always a fun experience and made me feel important. Those were outings that Mom and I did together. Everything about our shopping trip was special for me. New skates meant I was growing bigger and taller. A special achievement unto itself! The whiteness of the leather and the shininess of the blades added sensuality to my skating pleasure.

When my parents retired and moved to Florida, my mom gave me her ice skates to keep for her. Her skate bag and mine were on the bottom of a basement closet tucked away under a pile of blankets. When I finally found them many years later, the skate leather was cracked, dried, and crumbling on both our skates. Mother at the time was in her eighties. I sadly dumped both of our skating bags without ever telling her.

I did save her metal hook with the wooden handle used for tightening the laces. I put it next to my rusty metal roller skate key on its dirty white string. I wore this around my neck when I roller-skated on the cement sidewalks. They are both tucked away in a tan leather jewelry case that I received as a birthday gift when I was sixteen. Yes, I am sentimental, a saver of trinkets and a collector of all sorts of memorabilia.

My younger daughter, Leah, became the ice skater in our family. She would practice at a six a.m. patch session at the King of Prussia Ice Rink before school and sometimes after school. Her dad would drop her off at the rink. She could walk to her junior high and high school from the rink. Unfortunately, King of Prussia no longer has an ice-skating rink. After many transformations, that building has become the Upper Merion Senior Center.

Leah entered a number of ice-skating competitions. I, who never enjoyed sewing, sewed numerous tiny, shiny sequins on her new turtleneck, long-sleeved shirt and short, full, circular Danskin skirt to make a costume that sparkled in the spotlight for one of the special competitions she was in.

The sequins were small, shiny, and slippery with a tiny hole for stitching. The fabric was dense and elastic. Each stitch punctured the fabric. Because of my low vision, I used a needle threader to thread the needle with a silky thin thread. I had difficulty seeing the tiny hole in each individual sequin. They needed to be placed very close together. I had to continually repeat this process as I sewed each individual sequin in its place. The only time that I could work on this project was late at night after the children were in bed. It felt like this task was taking forever. However, listening to Johnny Mathis and Harry Belafonte as I sewed eased my angst. It was a slow, tedious process for me. But it was an intense labor of love.

During the competition, Leah's skating was graceful and precise. Her costume sparkled and twinkled in the spotlight as she did her routine. Her skirt flared out around her legs as she did her jumps and spins. I felt so proud of her as she took second place.

My Sage

During my adolescence, there was another older woman that I admired for her caring and organizational skills. I referred to her as My Sage. The rest of the world called her Eleanor Roosevelt. She was known for her desire to make the world a better place for all people. She worked to improve the lives of the underprivileged and discouraged racial discrimination.

Eleanor Roosevelt was the first honoree of Hadassah, Women's Zionist Organization of America to receive Hadassah's highest honor. She was the most notable world patron of Youth Aliyah. (The Hebrew word *aliyah* is defined as immigration of Jews from the diaspora to the land of Israel.) She established the Eleanor Roosevelt Youth Center in Beersheba.

I am proud to say that I am a third-generation life member of Hadassah. It is an organization in which I take a very active role.

Eleanor Roosevelt held a variety of titles. She was an American politician, diplomat, and activist as well as the longest-serving First Lady, acting in that capacity for twelve years. She also functioned as a delegate to the United Nations General Assembly.

I met Eleanor Roosevelt twice, not that she would ever have remembered. But to me they were special and historic moments. The first time we met, I was a camper at Camp Roosevelt, located near Hyde Park. She came to the camp and talked to us, and then she shook everybody's hand.

I can't say I remember anything she talked about. It was her warm and welcoming handshake, eye contact, and smile that I most remember. I also remember thinking of the contrast she presented. Such a famous and important woman coming to talk to a bunch of kids struck me as amazing. She was the paradox of a former First Lady, dressed in a plain cotton dress and sensible, comfy shoes. She could have passed for any camper's grandmother. I have a photograph of her in my camp scrapbook that I took with my Kodak Brownie camera.

The next time I saw Mrs. Roosevelt was a few years later, when a girlfriend and I were walking up 5th Avenue in New York City. Coming down the street facing us was an old lady in a heavy winter coat with a large beaver fur collar. She was carrying a large department store shopping bag in each hand. There were no guards or Secret Service people around her. My friend and I stopped in our tracks when we recognized her. We might have been pointing and giggling, as teenagers do. Mrs. Roosevelt smiled and said cheerfully, "Good morning, girls," and without even missing a step continued on her way. *We were awestruck!* We turned, and our gaze followed her until she disappeared around the corner.

Because I had seen Eleanor Roosevelt twice, I felt connected to her. She was much more important than a movie star. Eleanor was an independent thinker, a feminist who stood up for civil rights and was active in The League of Women Voters. As a past president of a local chapter of that civic-minded organization, I feel another connection to her. She became a role model and showed the world that women could be both effective and efficient at making positive changes in the world.

My mom was a "women's libber" before that title came into vogue. Mom worked because she wanted to, not because she needed to. Mom didn't see the need to be a homemaker when she could hire people to do that job. Louise, our cook and housekeeper, took very good care of our family. I thought of Louise as my second mother. Louise loved Robert and me as if we were her own children.

My mom, a teacher, was a good organizer and a people person. She took on leadership roles in volunteer organizations like Technion, Hadassah, and The League of Women Voters. I followed in her footsteps by being active and taking leadership roles in my own community.

Mary Margaret McBride

While my relationship with Eleanor Roosevelt could hardly be considered personal, I truly did have a personal connection with an actual celebrity. Mary Margaret McBride was a New York radio talk show hostess in the 1950s. My mom was on her radio program because my mom did the radio advertising for Messing Bakery. It was a well-known New York kosher bakery, owned and operated by my maternal grandfather and his younger brother. Mary Margaret had high standards and only advertised products that she approved of. She turned down tobacco and alcohol products. Messing Bakery was fortunate to be one of her advertisers

For me it is interesting and exciting to note that I knew two famous first ladies. I wish you to know that I, too, hold a title. I am the self-anointed Queen of King of Prussia. I even have a beautiful glittery crown.

Mary Margaret McBride was known as "The First Lady of Radio." She helped to lay the groundwork for Oprah, Terry Gross, Diane Rehm, and Sally Jessy Raphael. Mary Margaret McBride's popular radio show spanned more than forty years. She broadcasted from CBS, NBC, and ABC studios at different times during her career. Her audience was mostly housewives. She interviewed politicians, generals, movie stars, writers, gourmet chefs, and all types of celebrities. She also did freelance writing for *The Saturday Evening Post*, *Cosmopolitan*, and *Good Housekeeping*.

Below is a summary of what my 1954 diary had to say about a visit to Mary Margaret's studio. My diary was the leftover blank pages of a spiral notebook from my English class. I used old school notebooks because nobody would be interested to look through them. However, anything that looked like a diary could be tempting to read.

During the summer of 1954, Mom would take me along when she went to Manhattan to do a Messing Bakery commercial. That was the summer that Mom and Mary Margaret's relationship evolved into a personal friendship. We were sometimes invited to lunch at her place after the show. This day her radio guest was a doctor talking about the heart. In my journal I wrote:

The heart conversation was too heavy duty for me. I was too young for heart trouble, whether it be disease or boys.

Lunch on the other hand was delicious, especially dessert. There was a large bowl, which looked like it was filled with fresh fruit. However, the fruit was made of ice cream. Mary Margaret provided the dessert especially for me, so it was perfectly fine if I wanted a second helping. I did and enjoyed it as much as the first.

Mom reciprocated the luncheon invitations. Before Mary Margaret came the first time to our house, I spruced up my bedroom so I could show it to her. She liked my dolls and my goldfish. Mary Margaret occasionally sent me postcards when I was at summer camp and sent me and Robert delicious dark chocolate candy bars for the holidays. Yes, I wrote her thank you notes.

Here is a two-cent postcard she sent me that I saved. It was handwritten in her script. It arrived Tuesday, June 29, 1954, just before I went away to summer camp. It was addressed to:

Miss Zora Messing
125 Ocean Avenue
Brooklyn, New York

Dear Zora,

This is just to wish you a happy time in camp. I think of you often and wonder what you are doing. I think Mommy is wonderful on radio, and maybe I'll just turn it all over to her! Lots of love dear child, and have fun.

Mary Margaret

She also recommended books that she thought I might enjoy. I thought that she was a lovely lady. I knew she liked me. I had no idea, at that time, what a celebrity she was. To me she was Mom's and my friend who just happened to have a talk show on the radio. She asked me to call her Mary Margaret instead of Miss McBride because we were friends.

As a child, I tried not to attract the attention of adults. From my limited experience, many adults tended to be critical, especially if they were teachers. My mom was a teacher, and so were most of her friends. A casual conversation felt more like a quiz or an interrogation. "What books do you like to read?" "What do you like best about school?" My response was usually to shrug my shoulders and walk away, lest they try to convince me that I should like school.

My question was, "Why did they assume that I liked anything about books or school?" Though I sat in the front row and wore Coke-bottle-thick glasses, I couldn't read anything that was written on the blackboard. No teacher ever thought to write that material for me on a piece of paper or mimeograph it. Large-print textbooks and audiobooks didn't exist. There was no such thing as a teacher's aide who could help me.

Celebrities to me were a special category of adults. I had shaken hands with Mrs. Roosevelt. Her hand felt warm, dry, and friendly. The two times we briefly met, she spoke a few pleasantries to me, and I was close enough to her to look into her eyes. She noticed me, and for a few seconds I felt that I had her full attention. The feeling was indescribably delicious, WOW!

I didn't know until much later how famous Mary Margaret McBride was. All I knew and cared about was that she liked me. She liked to hug me, which I returned and enjoyed. She asked about me if I didn't accompany Mom. She was famous but a very down-to-earth, likable, and a reachable celebrity. That was probably why she had such a large radio audience.

Of the three celebrities—Tallchief, Henie, and Williams—who were the idols of my youth, the relationship was strictly admiration from afar. The short biographies I wrote about them seem like a school report. There was no personal connection, just a wish and a dream. Their talents were far beyond my capabilities. To me they represented the unattainable gold star.

However, Mary Margaret McBride was a personal acquaintance, at least by my teenage thinking. She made me feel acknowledged and important in her eyes.

Moving from these fringe relationships to my personal family, I met my future husband at summer camp when I was seventeen. After our first real conversation on a raft in the lake, I knew that he was someone special. I even wrote that in my camp diary back then. *Here is someone I have to get to know better.* Now after being married for fifty-seven years, I know him quite well, and I still think he is someone extremely special. Most of my friends admire his friendly, giving nature and helpfulness.

My Work

I never wished to become an athletic star like Maria, Sonja, and Esther, who I idealized. I wanted only their poise and grace of movement. Ice skating and swimming continue to hold a special fascination for me. I still swim; the other activities are merely spectator events now. I suspect my attraction to movement and posture led me to become a physical therapist and Alexander Technique teacher.

The Alexander Technique is a simple and practical method that helps to change habits in our daily activities. It improves ease and freedom of movement, coordination, and balance. It is a re-education of the mind and body rather than a series of exercises. The Alexander Technique helps a person discover a new balance in their body by releasing unnecessary tension. It can be applied to all activities of daily living: sitting, lying down, standing, walking, driving, and lifting. This technique is popular with both actors and athletes.

A physical therapist friend introduced me to the Alexander Technique (commonly known as Alexander) while we were working at the same facility. She had recently graduated from The Alexander School in Philadelphia. She kept talking to me about what a helpful addition this technique was to our PT skills. She kept putting her hands on me to demonstrate the technique. In the beginning I thought of it as hocus pocus. It seemed far removed from the medical model. However, she was persistent, and I was curious.

At first I felt nothing and was only aware of her hand placement. Whenever time allowed, she worked with me, explaining what was happening in my body physically and energetically. I gradually became aware and felt subtle postural changes in myself. I was standing taller and more erect. My head seemed balanced over my body rather than painfully forward. Consequently, I investigated the Alexander School and signed up for the three-year program. This was my first step into studying and using alternative modalities. It also opened my eyes to how I use my hands for seeing.

The female director of the Philadelphia School for the Alexander Technique helped me move from book learning to body learning. She came from a dance background and was an experienced Tai Chi practitioner. She was a terrific teacher with excellent personal relationship skills. She is considered a master teacher in the Alexander community.

Yes, I promised myself that I would *never ever* go back to any school again. I had my PT license! I rationalized: Alexander was body learning *not* book learning and written exams. I was now walking a new path of self-improvement. It was all about movement from my inside out. The learning and sensing my body's mobility was primarily for me and eventually to benefit my clients. I was able to attend weekday classes in the morning then hop the subway to work.

Many years later, I was teaching the Alexander Technique with a friend in London. We were in England attending an International Alexander Technique Conference. It was a large conference with students and teachers coming from New Zealand, Australia, Germany, Israel, Japan, and the United States. In addition to being a Certified Teacher of the Alexander Technique like me, my friend was also a skilled and certified riding instructor. At the end of the conference we were scheduled to teach an Alexander class for equestrians.

The night before the class we heard that Walter Carrington, an accomplished equestrian and an Alexander Technique patriarch, was going to be a student in our class. Walter had been a student of the founder of the technique, Frederick Matthias Alexander, affectionately referred to as FM. Walter continued the Alexander school for many years after Alexander's death. He also established a teacher's training program. You can imagine how excited and nervous this made us feel to have such a celebrity in our class. We chatted and giggled about this most of the night. Why would he want to take our class?

It turned out our "intelligence" had been a bit exaggerated. He wasn't attending our class; he was merely observing it. Nevertheless, we were quite thrilled to be in his company.

The next day we taught our workshop in an outside arena. The weather was perfect: cool and sunny. Walter sat on the wooden fence watching. We gave each rider a quick Alexander hands-on tune-up before they mounted. This helped attune them to their standing posture and breath. We then guided the equestrians riding their horses to move with ease and grace, through our hands-on or verbal instructions.

It was beautiful to watch the synchronicity between the horse and rider. The horses seemed to enjoy the lesson as much as the riders. Our class went well for the riders, their horses, and us.

Walter was very complimentary to us about his observations of the class and our teaching skills. He warmly shook both our hands and thanked us.

We flew home the next day feeling extremely honored and proud of ourselves. The conference and our workshop gave us lots of pleasant conversation on the plane ride home. We even planned our next Alexander Technique riders' workshop, which would be held at a Pennsylvania Dutch Barn.

Another teacher I admired was the last living student of FM Alexander. I met Elizabeth Walker when she was in her eighties. She came to the Philadelphia school, and I also studied with her at her home in Oxford, England. Her posture was comfortably erect. She was a skilled teacher, especially with her hands, who loved and lived what she taught. In her mid-eighties, she was still riding her two-wheeler bike around Oxford to do her errands. I found that impressive.

I am quickly approaching eighty. In Florida, for exercise, I peddle an adult tricycle. I do this for the walker's safety. The sidewalk and my tricycle are approximately the same width. The person walking must step off the path onto the grass, so I can pass. If we were both on the sidewalk together, I might accidentally ride over their toes because I have trouble visually gauging the distance between them and my back tires.

My next course of alternative study was CranioSacral Therapy (CST). I made plans with this same physical therapist to take an introductory course in CST in Manhattan. We could easily take the train or bus from Philadelphia to New York City. Lodging and meals would be at my parents' apartment in Brooklyn, a subway ride away. That made the trip cost effective. All we had to do was pay for the course. At the last moment, my therapist friend had to cancel, so I went alone.

Like the Alexander Technique, CranioSacral Therapy is another gentle, hands-on modality with which you can help yourself and others during times of stress, pain, or illness. The CranioSacral rhythm can be palpated anywhere on the body. It is another form of deep listening to the body.

During the class, I learned many different palpation skills and techniques. With each new exercise we changed partners. With each partner we role-played as the therapist and also as the client, then performing and receiving the treatment. This made me aware of the sensations felt by both the therapist and client.

As I worked with the students around the room, I learned that a small group of participants had also come from Philadelphia. I bonded with them and took many CST courses with them over the succeeding years. When at a class away from home, we always enjoyed meals and free time together.

The universe seemed to be taking charge of my alternate, hands-on education. As soon as I had free time, a new alternative class became available to me. I have usually let my intuition guide me. It is not something that I question. One of my clients told me I had powerfully energetic hands. She happened to be a Reiki Master. She insisted on teaching me the rudiments of Reiki.

I followed that up by taking a few Reiki classes. Over the succeeding years I took classes in a variety of alternative hands-on therapies. Thus, increasing the options for my clients' treatments. As well as receive healing benefits for myself.

Senior Citizen

At this point in my life, I enjoy spending six winter months in Florida, swimming, playing bridge and canasta, reading, attending courses, and taking care of myself. The warmer spring and summer months, I return to Pennsylvania and my home of fifty-three years. My life has balance and rhythm. Yet, I feel that I still don't know how to complete the sentence, "When I am older, I will…"

I still have much more growing and aging to do. Old is a mindset, not a particular number. There are many forty- and fifty-year-olds who think and act old. Living in a Florida retirement community, I realize that I am what is now called the new middle age. I am surrounded by many late-eighty- and ninety-year-olds who are fully functional mentally and physically. They have become my idols and role models.

A physically fit ninety-seven-year-old gentleman friend of mine survived the Holocaust while living in concentration camps because he could fix bikes and had his own set of tools. He was an intelligent, kind, caring, stately, widowed gentleman.

I asked him one day to take a look at my tricycle because it was making a loud, annoying, clanking noise. This man spent over three hours working outside on my bike in the hot Florida sun with my husband by his side. He was bending, squatting, and even rode the bike to test it out. He really was enjoying what he was doing. Herm and I were both very impressed with his stamina. To look at him in action, you never would have guessed his age. He is definitely a role model for us. I wave at his house and ring my bell when I ride my bike down his street.

Fortunately, longevity has been in my family's history. My maternal great-grandfather lived until ninety-two. We called him Little Grandpa because he was short and stocky. When we visited him, we usually sat around his circular dining room table with a terrarium sitting in the center on a hand-crocheted lace tablecloth. I was given cookies to nibble on. The one thing I remember him telling me was, "Don't talk while eating fish. You might choke on a bone." As a six-year-old, I knew that wouldn't happen to me because I didn't eat fish. It was too smelly.

Three of my four grandparents lived into their eighties. My father who was twelve years older than my mother lived to be eighty-two. My mother passed away just two months short of her ninety-fifth birthday. It is my hope that the family longevity gene has been passed down to me and my brother.

When I became a senior citizen or crone at age sixty-five, I gave myself a year of mental, physical, religious, spiritual, and fundraising challenges to complete. My friends had no interest in challenging themselves at this time of their lives. I would only be competing against myself. So I knew I would be a winner!

Winning had not been something that happened often in my life. I scheduled the year down to the finish line with a large party at Tavern on the Green for my sixty-sixth birthday to celebrate all my accomplishments.

Though the word *crone* may have a negative connotation to some, I see her as a wise, strong, independent woman, a free thinker, and a person who makes positive changes in her world.

For my seventy-fifth birthday, I decided to write a memoir for several reasons.

1. It would be cathartic for me.
2. I believe that I have an important message for parents, teachers, therapists, religious leaders, and coaches. Watch out for the unintentional hurtful words and actions you use, especially when working with children. Children internalize so much.
3. I am on a campaign against labeling. In today's world it is also called bullying. One of the groups

that I feel is most hurt by labeling is the disabled. So my motto is: Let's "dis" the "dis" in disability. And what do you get? **ABILITY!** Learn to see the person beyond what is physically visible: crutches, braces, wheelchair, limp, or deformity!

Only now am I beginning to see my accomplishments and acknowledging them. I have made my mark in this world, and I am not finished yet. As a crone, wise woman, or elder, it is my time for giving back, teaching the lessons of life that I have learned to anyone who cares to listen. Like the Dalai Lama, age hasn't stopped me from giggling and being playful.

Now my days seem even busier than when I was raising a family and working. But included in each day now is ME TIME: a time to meditate, reflect, stare into space, journal, write gratitude and self-acknowledgment lists, do tai chi, or just be alone with my thoughts. I still have a lot more living to do.

As a physical therapist, I enjoyed working in a variety of different environments: large and small hospitals, nursing homes, and rehabilitation centers. It was modern technology that forced me to open a private practice in my home. The computer at the nurse's station became the new receptacle for patient notes that used to be handwritten in patients' charts. For most people, computer print was easier to read than handwritten notes. However, this caused a big problem for me.

I was used to working with a desktop computer at home. The multi-person, shared computer was too far back on the desk, and the print was too small for me to decipher. I was not sure how to handle this situation. I certainly wasn't going to talk about not being able to see the printed words on the computer. I wasn't going to disclose my visual problem to my coworkers. Even at this point in my life, I was still controlled by my secret.

After two weeks of avoiding this new note-taking system, I made up a story about an elderly sick, widowed aunt who was coming to my home from the hospital after a stroke. She had been living alone but now was unable to care for herself. I needed to be home with her. With that story, it was easy to leave that job on good terms.

I began planning my private practice. I knew a few doctors who would refer patients to me. Our library/ guest room in the basement would be a perfect physical therapy office. There was a bathroom next door. Our friendly black lab, Baxter, greeted my patients as they entered through the side door into our comfortable and spacious recreation room. This became a waiting room.

Many people wandered around this room examining and enjoying my many different telephones and phone equipment on display. One of my many hobbies is collecting antique telephones. They are displayed throughout my house.

One wall of my physical therapy office was lined with bookcases on top of sliding door cabinets that my husband built. PT books filled these shelves along with books on holistic health, antiques (especially Victorian furniture), Israel, paperback novels, and Herman's college engineering textbooks. In front of Herman's books, I displayed many of Zora Neal Hurston's books. I wanted my clients to see my name, ZORA, in print. I did that a long time before I had any ideas about being an author. Was that a sign for my future self that I would write a book?

Across this spacious room from the bookcase were three large, square windows overlooking the patio and tree-shaded backyard. The valances above the windows were seven colorful thirteen-by-fifteen-inch cloth, rectangular chakra flags. Chakras are the seven energy centers of the body: 1. red/root, 2. orange/sacral, 3. yellow/solar plexus, 4. green/heart, 5. blue/throat, 6. indigo/third eye, 7. violet-white/crown. These flags added color and a vibrant energy to the room.

The walls were paneled in a simulated-wood pattern. The floor was carpeted. A velour-covered sleeper couch with a modern geometric design sat under the windows. The room was a homey therapy gym. The far back wall had a large standard treadmill against it. Catty-corner across the room was a large Soloflex machine which my clients used for many purposes such as toning, stretching and strengthening muscles, cardiovascular fitness, balance, and coordination.

There was a DP BodyTone machine which was also a multigym for a small office. As a rowing machine, clients exercised their thighs, arms, shoulders, backs, and waists. This machine adapted so that one could do squats, bench presses, curls, shoulder presses, and shoulder shrugs. The nice thing about it was that it folded up for easy storing. Hand weights were racked on the wall.

Near the hand weights was a small, decorative metal, free-standing square shelf covered with toys, balls, and stuffed animals. The children especially loved playing with my rotary dial Minnie and Mickey Mouse telephones. Rolling around the room were a variety of colored, different-sized, blown-up exercise balls. When needed, I opened a folding massage table that would stand in the center of the room. One corner wall displayed my diplomas.

In front of the treadmill were two signs at eye level. One was a six-inch red circle that could be worn as a pin. It read in large, white print:

I'm In No Shape To Exercise

The second sign was framed in a nine-by-twelve white, narrow-plastic picture frame. It was titled PHYSICAL FITNESS.

> *I strongly believe in exercise and manage to get all I need by jumping to conclusions, flying off the handle, dodging responsibility, skipping work, bouncing checks, fighting progress, dragging my heels, and pushing my luck.*

I find humor an asset to exercising. When you smile or laugh, you are using your facial muscles; your body and breath tend to relax.

On another wall was a framed oil painting of rolling ocean waves. The artist was my mother. This picture seemed to capture the ebb and flow of movement that occurred in this home physical therapy office.

When I was up north in Pennsylvania, I defined myself by my occupation. I am a holistic manual physical therapist with a clinic in my home. Holistic meaning, I treat the whole patient, taking into account their mental, emotional, and social factors along with physical symptoms. I include a number of hands-on techniques in my treatments.

I specialized in treating children with delayed development and adults with chronic pain issues. I was highly specialized and skilled at what I did. I loved my work and the people I worked with. We both benefited by our shared experience. I retired in June 2012. If pressed for more information about myself, I proudly say I am a mother of three and a grandmother of six. The world still holds females in these traditional roles.

Positive Self-Talk

Self-talk makes us who we are. It expresses how we think about ourselves, interact with others, and view the world. It impacts self-esteem, confidence, and self-image. Noticing how we talk about ourselves is the beginning of change for the better. When trying to change, be mindful of sarcastic, critical, pessimistic expressions you use to describe others or yourself. Putting ourselves down never feels good.

Whether you think you can,
or think you can't, you are right.
– Henry Ford

Positive, constructive self-talk:

1. Boosts confidence. Successful people believe in themselves. Psychologists believe that confidence is most important to personal and professional success. Introduce optimistic thoughts like "I can do this." "I'm good at that."

2. According to the American Heart Association, positive self-talk can help control stress. As a result, it makes you feel calmer and less anxious.

3. It helps you improve your performance in anything you do. Self-talk is an important part of sport and acting psychology. It helps athletes and actors reduce pre-jitters and performance anxieties. Self-talk isn't just for athletes and actors. It is also important for professional and personal success.

4. Do daily optimistic dialog with yourself so you become the master of your thoughts. *I can do this. I am confident of my knowledge.*

5. Listen to yourself to identify negative words or thoughts.

6. Change words. Inner voices tend to be negative core beliefs, old ideas about ourselves that lurk in our subconscious mind. These beliefs tend to fit into three categories: helplessness, unworthiness, or unlovability.

7. Write down your negative inner conversation. See the words in black and white.

Action Exercise

Keep a journal for at least a week in which you write your answer to these questions.

- What is one of your typical negative thoughts?
- How do you feel when you have this negative thought?
- What facts do you know that tells you this isn't true?
- State a positive true thought.
- How does this make you feel?

CHAPTER 2

Life's Influences

Healing is a path of self-discovery!

Zora the PT

My first professional position as a physical therapist was in a rehab center. I was working with two young women patients who both had tragic, life-altering consequences from their childbirth experiences. The impact on me personally was profound. My original expectation going into physical therapy was that I'd be treating people with ailments such as a stroke, neck, and back injuries, sports- and work-related injuries, chronic conditions like arthritis, and post-op orthopedic problems. I had not envisioned that there would be situations where previously healthy young women would become permanently disabled as a result of simply giving birth.

As a consequence, I postponed my plans for starting a family; I began exploring natural childbirth which had not yet come back into vogue. I was so frightened by what had happened to these two young mothers that I read every nursing textbook on childbirth I could get my hands on. I was aware of all manner of complications that could occur. An improperly inserted needle during an epidural could cause permanent paralysis. Anesthesia improperly administered could lead to irreversible cognitive or physical disabilities.

I also researched obstetricians. I found an OBGYN at my hospital who was known to perform natural deliveries. Natural childbirth was not a common procedure at that time. He did imply that most of the hospital staff preferred putting the mother out during delivery. He agreed to take me on as a patient so I could have a natural delivery. All of this occurred far in advance of my actually becoming pregnant.

My Children

With my first child, I worked up until the week I was due. I hadn't told anyone at work I was pregnant until my eighth month. Then I fudged how far along I really was so that I could continue working.

Prior to my announcement, a female physician whose office was between the physical therapy gym and the bathroom, stopped me one afternoon. With a twinkle in her eye, she asked me if I had anything to tell her. I looked directly at her, shook my head and replied, "Not for another month or so." We both smirked, and she never disclosed my secret.

How did she know? Was it my frequent bathroom trips, or had she heard me retching? To cover that sound I turned both sink faucets on full force and frequently flushed the toilet.

Vomit and being nauseated are things I do not handle well. So wouldn't you know that most of the patients I was treating in the gym at that time had cancer. As I helped them stand up in the parallel bars, they would get queasy and or nauseated. I had just enough time to reseat them and make sure they were safe before I ran to the bathroom. When I became a parent, I wasn't even able to take care of my own children if they threw up. I ended up joining them over the opened toilet.

My water broke as I was walking across my bedroom carpet the night before my due date. It was January. I was wearing heavy sweatpants that quickly became soaked as did the rug below me. I stood there dumbfounded. I decided I needed to change my clothes and headed for the closet. My husband, Herm, who is usually calm, cool, and collected, grabbed me before I had taken two steps, wrapped a blanket around me, and practically carried me to the car. He had no intention of delivering this baby. He ran back for my packed suitcase, and off we drove to the hospital with me in my cold, soggy, wet, sweatpants.

I was very grateful to the doctor I had selected to bring my first baby into the world. When I was on the delivery table, he was extremely gentle and explained every step of the process. He let me wear my glasses in the OR, and he even carefully angled the mirror so I had a view of the area where the action was taking place.

The baby slid out after pushing harder than I had ever thought possible. The doctor carefully picked up the baby and showed her to me as he announced,

"Zora, you have a beautiful daughter." He handed her off to the pediatric nurse and then asked me to push again. Being thrilled and in a euphoric state I excitedly yelled, "I'm having twins!" The doctor laughed and said, "With all your reading, Zora, you forgot about the afterbirth." I then burst out crying, "You mean I'm not having twins?" The nurses in the OR were giggling at this overreaction. I was embarrassed at the time but later came to realize that it was my hormones and the intensity of this thrilling and wonderful event.

Our pediatrician gave us some advice before taking baby Amy home from the hospital. If she cries there are three things to consider:

1. She has soiled her diaper.
2. A safety pin is pricking her (No need to worry about this anymore).
3. She is hungry.

We drove the short distance home with Amy on my lap in the front seat. This was prior to seatbelts and infant car seats. We entered our apartment for the first time as parents. I gingerly placed Amy down on the brown couch as we removed our heavy winter coats. Everything seemed serene, calm, and comfortable.

Then as we were admiring our baby, she started to cry. We looked at each other with a slight moment of panic. Then we went through the three possibilities. Her diaper was changed, and the safety pins were securely closed. We figured it must be the third issue. I nursed her, and she happily fell asleep in my arms.

Those were such wonderful and simple moments of serenity. We survived the first day as parents at home and believed things would go easy until she became a teenager. So much for our early parenting knowledge; it is a learn-as-you-go kind of job.

Our second daughter was born three years later during a heavy December snowstorm. All week Herm had parked our car at the top of the driveway so that it would be easy to get out when we needed to. Our three-year-old daughter was asleep in her crib. We had just spoken to Herm's parents, saying nothing was happening yet for me.

Once we hung up the phone, my contractions started. I called my best friend who lived nearby to come get Amy. We would most likely be heading to the hospital that evening. I wanted to wait awhile, and Herm wanted to go as soon as Amy was picked up. Herm was worried about the snowy, icy roads, and he certainly didn't want to deliver this baby.

As time passed, the snow became heavier and the roads more slippery.

I made a deal with Herm. I would leave for the hospital on one condition. We would wait downstairs in the lobby until I felt it was time to go up to the delivery room. He was not happy with this, but he didn't have any choice. He put my bag in the car. I walked in a zigzag path up the steep, snow-filled driveway with Herm supporting and gently pushing me from behind. I finally made it covered in a wet, white blanket, huffing and puffing with my breath crystallizing in front of me. This would have made a memorable photograph, a Kodak Moment.

It was a dark night with only a few cars on the road. We progressed slowly because the snow was drifting on the road as it descended from above. The roads were slippery. There was little traffic, but we crawled our way to the hospital safely. Herm deposited me on a bench in the lobby while he parked the car and then brought my suitcase in. We waited about two hours on that bench before I felt it was time to go up to the delivery floor. I occasionally dozed or walked around. Herm read. The hospital night watchman kept checking on me each time he made his rounds.

Upon arriving upstairs to the delivery area, the floor nurse called my OB doctor. He lived too far away from the hospital to make it on time for my impending delivery. So they called the on-call doctor who happened to live close to the hospital. This doctor was in a foul mood as he entered the OR where I was lying on the table with my feet already in the stirrups prepared to deliver.

This doctor didn't bother to introduce himself to me. His manner was rough and gruff and made me feel that I was simply a "pregnancy" and not even a human being. The OR staff seemed to be standing tensely at attention awaiting his commands. From the doctor's reaction and whispering of the nurses, I knew that something was terribly amiss.

I calmly asked them to please tell me what was happening. They acted as though I didn't exist. This scared me even more. All of a sudden there was an anesthesiologist at my head with a mask in his hand. I was about to go into panic mode and scream. Somehow, I made my voice sound calm. I looked into the anesthesiologist eyes and said firmly, "I am having this child naturally!"

I looked at the doctor and nurses and said, "You are scaring me by not telling me what is wrong." No one responded. I felt hands inside me and heard soft mumbled words from the doctor. Once again I appealed to the anesthesiologist and said, "Nobody is listening to me. If you put that mask on me, I will sue. Please just tell me what is happening, and I will cooperate."

The anesthesiologist whispered in my ear that the baby was breech (feet first) and the cord was around the baby's neck. One leg was already hanging out of me. They were trying to turn the baby, but it wasn't happening. The anesthesiologist kept the mask in his hand but didn't put it on my face. He seemed to be the only one who was listening to my concerns. I didn't want to be put out. I told him that I had a high pain tolerance, and I wanted this child to have a natural birth like my first child.

This delivery had been a frightening and unpleasant experience. But I had managed to be awake through the whole thing. I thanked the anesthesiologist for listening to me. He said he thought I was very brave.

After the baby was cleaned up, they gave her to me. Holding this tiny, beautiful, strong baby helped me let go of some of the angst and frustration I felt during delivery.

That's when my doctor finally arrived at the delivery room. He missed all the action, and I sorely missed his gentility and on-going explanations of what was happening instead of being frightened and ignored. The doctor and nurses worked on me as though I was just a "thing" not a rational human being.

Herm followed the doctor into the OR to meet his new daughter, Leah. That's when all became right again.

Our baby boy arrived ten years later. My childhood dream became a reality. All of my children have grown to be accomplished adults. They have given me six marvelous grandchildren. What more could I ask for?

A New Bathrobe

Prior to Adam's birth, before we told anyone we were pregnant, I "mentioned" to my mother-in-law that I needed a new bathrobe. It took her a few moments before her face registered understanding and she asked, "Are you telling me something?" I smiled as I replied, "Yes!"

Both times I had been pregnant, she had made me a long, cozy, warm, velvet bathrobe.

My favorite robe was the first one, a full-length, quilted red velour A-line with a belt. It had a high-neck mandarin collar. The buttons down the front were ornate large, round, rib-textured metal. I always felt regal wearing it. I wore it until the elbow and seat areas were threadbare. I managed to save the buttons. Many years later, Mom made me a simpler pattern red-velvet bathrobe with white lace down the front and around the neck which I still have today. Red is a color that complements my complexion and makes me feel warm and happy.

From the scraps of material leftover from my first red, quilted robe, my mother-in-law made a Victorian doll's dress and matching wide-brimmed hat. The dress had a scooped neck, three-quarter length sleeves, and a sweepingly wide floor-length, A-line skirt. The dress was completely lined in white linen. Circling the base of the skirt was a two-inch width of delicate-patterned lace with a curved edge. This lace draped around the front of the dress forming an apron effect. Lace also draped like a scarf around the dress's collar. On the back of the dress was a fluffy, three-tiered lace bustle. The skirt was supported by a stiff, wallpaper crinoline.

The outfit was offset by the wide-brimmed hat. She sewed a bouquet of colorful mini felt flowers on the right, and a small pearl hatpin secured the hat to the brunette doll. Under her clothing, the doll was secured to an upright kitchen paper towel holder to give her balance, support, and height.

I keep this doll on a small, round marble-top Victorian wooden table beside our upright player piano at the entrance to what we lovingly call our parlor (living room in the modern vernacular). She complements the room's plush red carpet, red-velour rippled valance, and red tie-back drapes over sheer white-lace curtains.

All my children were winter babies, so my bathrobes were warm velvet. Mom also made me a long, straight, floral-cotton, zipper-front robe for the warmer months.

Though I rarely wear bathrobes these days, all the bathrobes she made me are still hanging in my closet some fifty years later. I can't part with them. I love just touching them. They fill me with love and happy memories.

Mind Mapping

What are you wishing to birth? Is there a project you've been thinking about starting? Here's an easy way to begin. Follow the mind-mapping approach.

Mind mapping is a pictorial form of outlining. It is a diagram used to visually organize information. It is hierarchical and shows relationships among the pieces of the whole. Mind mapping organizes ideas and concepts.

Action Exercise

You will need blank paper and colored pens or pencils.

In the center of a sheet of blank paper, write your major thought or topic. Keep it brief. Encircle it with a bold or bright color. Branches flow from the center to sub themes.

Each subtopic level can be encircled in its own color. They too will have subtopics.

Carry this paper around with you for a week or longer, jotting down all thoughts as they come to you.

When you feel there is nothing more you can add, put this information into a story.

See the diagram on the next page for mind mapping.

A Mind Map

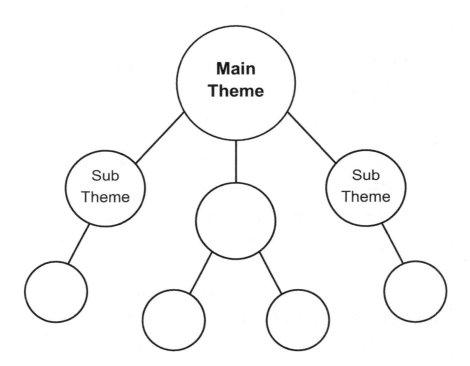

CHAPTER 3

From Brooklyn to King of Prussia

My dreams manifest into reality every day.

My Neighborhood

My home from birth until I got married was a two-bedroom apartment on the first floor of a six-story building in Brooklyn. We even had a tree growing out of the cement sidewalk in front of my parents' bedroom window. This always reminded me of the book, *A Tree Grows in Brooklyn* by Betty Smith. I cried as I read this book and also when I saw the movie because it touched my heart. It was the struggle of an immigrant Irish family. I was fortunate to be born a second-generation American.

Our apartment was well located. Prospect Park was directly across the street from us. On the corner street, Lincoln Road, was the BMT subway (Prospect Park station), a newsstand/candy store, a local grocery store, a kosher butcher, a dry cleaner, a chain grocery store, and a drug store. Everything that we needed was located within a short walking distance from our home.

One block farther was busy Flatbush Avenue with buses, a movie theater, and more shops and restaurants. We were within walking distance of Ebbets Field—Dodgers Stadium. It seemed that everyone in Brooklyn was a Dodger fan.

The Dodgers

If the Dodgers were playing, my family was glued to the ten-inch TV screen. My head was usually blocking everybody's view because I sat close to follow the action. We had only this one TV. It was in the corner by a side window in my parents' bedroom. A TV was a prize possession in those days. When the World Series was on and the Dodgers were playing, this TV was on, even if no one was in the room. My father would come in to watch between dental patients. Louise, our cook/

housekeeper, was an avid Dodger fan. She would be constantly in and out of this room to keep my father and his patients updated on the score.

When I was a child of seven or eight, I went to a night game with my parents and brother, Robert. We walked to Ebbets Field and then climbed the steep metal steps to find seats in the bleachers. I was exhausted before the game even started. A boisterous crowd of Brooklyn fans filled the seats. The field was brightly lit. I wished I had my sunglasses with me. Venders with hot dogs, soda, beer, ice cream, popcorn, and candy loudly hawked their wares as they clanked up and down the steps. Dad bought us hot dogs, chips, and sodas, a special treat for dinner. Robert and I ate and drank our way through the game.

It was a hot summer night. I was wearing a brand-new striped one-piece romper with spaghetti straps that tied on my shoulders. My dad told me I looked very cute. I thought so too.

Some men drinking beer sat in the row behind us. One of the men dropped his can of beer. It showered my back and drenched my new outfit. I was chilled and smelled like a brewery. It made me feel damp, sticky, stinky, and yucky. Even dessert didn't make me feel better, although I finished it. When the game was over, it was late. "Dah Bums," the Dodger's nickname, had won! Hurray! I was so tired that Dad carried me home.

The Dodgers left Brooklyn on May 28, 1957, for Los Angeles, California. It was a sad, sad day. From that day on, I stopped watching sports on television.

The Zoo

As a child I frequently visited the Brooklyn Zoo in Prospect Park. I first would watch the elephants in their outside cage. They were huge and majestic. Their trunks could do so many things. I especially liked when they used it to give themselves a shower or tenderly nudge their offspring.

Leaving the elephants, we came to the big cats. There was one visit to the lion's cage that I will never forget because it was both scary and humorous. A large male with a full mane was roaring and shaking his head as he walked in circles around his cage. A big crowd had gathered in front to see what the roaring was all about. The lion came close to the front bars, stared at the people, then raised his leg and sprayed the crowd. Luckily, I was not in the direct line of fire. I guess he was pissed at the crowd.

Then it was off to see the quiet, sedate zebras. A welcome respite from the roaring lions! As I walked, I nibbled on Crackerjacks. When the box was finished, I put the prize in my pocket and then turned the box upside down so the crumbs would float down to the pavement. I quickly stepped out of the way as the pigeons dive-bombed into the area for their snack.

The Butcher Shop

I remember the butcher shop because of its smell, temperature, and the clucking chickens on Fridays. The sawdust-covered floor felt slippery. The store was long and narrow with a refrigerated showcase usually filled with raw meat. When I pressed my face against the chilled glass, my breath would fog it up.

Friday mornings, baby carriages and strollers would be parked outside. The women would be lined up against the counter chatting as they waited to buy their meat for Shabbat dinner. Their children slipped and slid in the sawdust or tossed it at each other. We could hear the live chickens clucking in the back before they were ritually slaughtered.

One day, a headless chicken escaped and ran through the store. The women were screaming hysterically as they grabbed their children and ran out the door. I can recall that scene so vividly with all its sights, smells, and sounds, even though it happened when I was ten or eleven years old.

My Friends in the Apartment House

My parents moved in when this building was brand new. They lived there for almost forty years. My father's dental office was a second apartment attached to our living space. My mom brought me from the hospital to this home. My brother, Robert, was three years older and was eager to meet and greet me. So was Louise.

My very first friends were the children in this building. We would sit on the front stoop and play marbles, pick up sticks, or hand-clapping games as we recited silly rhymes like "Miss Mary Mac, Mac, Mac. All dressed in black, black, black." When we had chalk, we would play potsy by throwing a stone into a numbered box which we chalked on the sidewalk. Then we would hop on one foot around the boxes in numerical order to pick up the stone. Jumping rope as we repeated jingles was also a fun pastime. We could do this for hours or until we were called for dinner. This same group of children would be together in the early morning as we waited for our school buses.

As we matured, we girls gathered on the roof for sunbathing. We wore our bathing suits or shorts and halter tops. We enjoyed parading around like we were in the Miss America pageant. We would bring up beach chairs or blankets and tons of snacks and soda. Of course, we lathered ourselves up with baby oil and sat with tinfoil reflectors around our head and shoulders to catch every bit of the sun's rays possible. A portable, battery-operated radio blasted popular songs that we frequently sang along with. Our time was spent gossiping about the neighbors, movie stars, hairstyles, makeup, and anything else that popped into our heads.

As a teenager, a girlfriend from the building and I would sit on the stairs between the apartment floors and smoke cigarettes. In those days, everybody smoked— even your doctor. The magazine ads said, "More doctors smoke Camels than any other brand." This was a time when smoking was cheap and socially acceptable. Hollywood stars like John Wayne advertised Camels.

Both our mothers smoked, so it was easy to get cigarettes. My mother smoked Philip Morris. They came in a round metal can. My friend's mother smoked a filtered cigarette which came in a flip-top cardboard box. I can't remember the brand name. We knew not to steal from a new pack or a nearly-empty pack. Taking one or two cigarettes from a half-full pack would be far less noticeable.

Blowing smoke rings or long trailing exhales like the glamorous movie stars was always fun. We both became very skilled at that. If we heard the elevator stop on the floor we were lounging on, we would race one flight either up or down the staircase. Before heading home, we went out on the roof to air our clothes and chew some gum. We were never caught, thank goodness!

I smoked in college and continued when I was married. It made me feel grown-up. A pack could last me two weeks or longer. Herm was a nonsmoker. On very rare occasions, he might smoke a cigar if given one. I hated the smell of cigars. One day Herm brought home a cigar. He said, "I won't smoke this in the house if you won't smoke in the house." Since I was only a social smoker, I found it easy to give up cigarettes. My mom also gave up smoking as reports of smoking's ill effects on health kept surfacing. My father never smoked.

During the summers when we were young, my parents always sent Robert and me away to camp in the country. They wanted to get us out of the hot city because they were afraid of us contracting polio. One of the little girls in our apartment building did succumb to polio during the summer. When I returned from camp, she was in a child's wheelchair with long metal braces on both legs. She did not seem to be her happy, carefree self anymore.

I was impressed by the young nurse pushing her wheelchair. The nurse was all in white, wearing a crisply starched uniform, white stockings, white laced-oxford shoes, and white cap over her brunette hair. I think the crispness of the uniform made more of an impression on me then the poor little girl in the wheelchair. That's when I decided to become a nurse.

My dream of wearing a pristine white uniform was shattered when I told my father I wanted to be a nurse. His reply was typical for his generation. "No daughter of mine is cleaning bedpans!" That ended that conversation before it even began.

College

Adelphi College in Garden City, Long Island accepted me as a student but not in the nursing program. That was smart on their part because I couldn't see to read a thermometer. During college, I lived in the dormitory. To me, it was pretty much like camp except I had only one roommate. I could be home in an hour by taking the Long Island Railroad and the subway. Or I could catch a ride to Brooklyn with one of the many commuting students.

I thought I had so much freedom at college even though we had a ten o'clock weekday curfew, twelve a.m. on Friday nights, and one a.m. on Saturday nights.

My children and grandchildren laughed at the idea of curfews for college students.

We had to sign in and out if we left the campus. When I had a date, I had to write his name in the sign-out book. Dates always tried to look over your shoulder to see who else you were dating. I quickly learned how to cover the last entry with my right hand as I signed out with my left.

Many weekends I went home to Brooklyn because I was already dating my future husband. Our first home was a small apartment in West Philadelphia, for I was Mrs. Natanblut at that point. That, however, is a long story about how I got from here to there.

The summer between my junior and senior years in high school I volunteered at a local hospital in the physical therapy (PT) and occupational therapy (OT) Departments. PT was a recognized profession. OT was just getting started and was not a profession at that point. I perceived OT as teaching arts and crafts. I like doing crafts, not teaching them. The head of the PT department took me under his wing and sold me on what a terrific profession physical therapy was for a young woman like me.

I graduated from Adelphi College in January. I was accepted at Columbia Physician and Surgeon's

PT program for the following September. What was I to do for the intervening six months?

An Adelphi girlfriend and I decided we would go to Israel until school started in the fall. That idea didn't go far because she found out that her graduate work-study program in social work began right away. I knew that I wasn't going to Israel or anywhere by myself.

Herm had graduated from Cooper Union with a degree in electrical engineering the previous June. He had taken a job with General Electric and was already living and working in Philadelphia. He came back to Brooklyn most weekends to be with me.

Marriage

Herman made an appointment with my father to ask for my hand in marriage. He and Dad were sitting in the living room talking. Mom and I were in the bathroom combing our hair with the door ajar, trying to listen to their conversation. They talked about the weather, football, soccer, basketball, baseball, especially the Brooklyn Dodgers, Herm's job, and all sorts of other small talk topics.

Finally, my father helped the conversation progress by asking Herm, "Do you have something to ask me?"

Of course, my father's answer was an enthusiastic, "YES!" My parents already loved Herman.

Herm gave me a beautiful diamond engagement ring in November. We had been pinned for a year prior to that. Pinning meant he had given me his fraternity pin to wear, and we had a committed relationship. We got married on February 25, 1962, a month after I graduated from college. That ended Herm's long weekend commutes from Philadelphia to Brooklyn.

Here is what the *New York World-Telegram and Sun* wrote about our wedding.

Miss Messing Is Wed to Herman Natanblut

Miss Zora Estelle Messing, daughter of Dr. and Mrs. Arthur Isaacs, of Brooklyn became the bride of Herman Bernard Natanblut, son of Mr. and Mrs. Milton Natanblut, also of Brooklyn. The ceremony was performed Sunday by Rabbi Abraham Kelman and Rabbi Benjamin Krietman at the Brooklyn Jewish Center.

The bride wore a gown of candlelight satin trimmed with Alençon lace at the scooped neckline and bodice and panels of the skirt and chapel train. Her veil was a mantilla of Brussels princess lace.

She carried white orchids, stephanotis and lilies of the valley.

Miss Faye Natanblut, sister of the bridegroom, was maid of honor. The bridesmaids were Miss Lucy Blake and Judith Goodman. Robert Messing, brother of the bride, was best man. Mrs. Natanblut is a granddaughter of David Leon Messing, president of the former Messing Bakeries of Brooklyn. Her surname was legally changed from Isaacs to Messing. The bride received her bachelor's degree at Adelphi College.

The bridegroom is with General Electric in Philadelphia where he is working for his master's degree in electrical engineering at the University of Pennsylvania.

The couple will make their home in Philadelphia.

We chose the date February 25, 1962, because that was when my rabbi was free and the Eastern Parkway Jewish Center was available. It was a big, beautiful synagogue. It even had a swimming pool. For a number of years, our large Messing clan celebrated Thanksgiving there, so we knew the food was delicious.

My mom did all the planning for the wedding because I was busy studying and taking final exams. She was in her glory being the wedding planner. She and Dad got married during the Depression. I know nothing about my parents' wedding but assume it was small. I do know, however, they took a train ride across the USA for a honeymoon.

My wedding was a lavish affair. Another childhood dream come true. All I did was pick my bridal gown, the music, and give Mom my guest list. She saw to the invitations, the menu, the décor, the emcee, the band, and all the other large and small details. She was a very good organizer. My Uncle David Brietbard had beautiful penmanship. He calligraphed the invitations and place cards.

Everything at the wedding went smoothly. To this day, almost sixty years later, I still say it was the best wedding I ever attended. I smiled and laughed so much that day that my facial muscles ached. Thanks Mom and Dad!

After the wedding as we left the synagogue, there were two police cars waiting outside. A policeman asked if we wanted a send-off. Of course we said, "YES!" One police car drove in front of our lavishly decorated car. The other police car drove behind our car. We slowly drove from the synagogue to my house to change clothing before going on our honeymoon. The police cars' sirens were blaring as their lights were flashing. People in cars honked their horns and waved at us. I felt like a queen for the day, and I was floating on cloud nine.

We honeymooned for a week at Grossinger's Hotel in the Catskills. For dinner, we were seated at a table with two other honeymooning couples. Two very funny things happened as we approached our dinner table. First, Herm introduced me by saying, "This is my wife, Zora Messing," a name he was used to calling me. We had been married only a day. Then one of the other husbands at our table and I burst out laughing. We knew each other because we had dated in the past. Isn't that an odd coincidence? We both found this situation humorous, but his bride did not.

Homes in Pennsylvania

My next home was Herm's student bachelor apartment in West Philadelphia. It was a one-bedroom apartment on the top floor of an old house on 38th Street and Spruce and was right in the midst of the college housing. The location was great, but the décor left much to be desired. We couldn't move until the spring when school let out and apartments became available.

It was a furnished apartment with overstuffed, mismatched, stained, old furniture. All three rooms were small. The kitchen was narrow with a small table and two chairs. To open the refrigerator door, I had to slide the table and chairs to the left. I slid the table and chairs to the right to open the oven door. All the appliances were old and not well cared for.

The bathroom was one step lower than the rest of the apartment. It had a lovely, large antique clawfoot bathtub. In my opinion, it was the nicest thing in the apartment. It was a big step down to get out of the tub. The only storage space in the apartment was two large shelves behind the tub which was protected by a plastic shower curtain. The place had one tiny closet in the bedroom. A short while after we moved out, this building and the other buildings on the block were torn down to make way for a new graduate dormitory. Fortunately, we only had to stay there for a few months. When school let out for summer break in June, I went apartment hunting. Apartment hunting became a serious job.

Being married and living in Philadelphia made going to Columbia in New York impossible. So I quickly applied to the University of Pennsylvania, School of Allied Medicine in the physical therapy program. My transcript from Adelphi got lost in the mail twice. Can you believe that? I finally went to Adelphi, picked up my transcript in a double-sealed envelope, and hand-delivered it to the administrator of the Penn PT school. I had been verbally accepted, but they needed my official transcript.

Herman and I were both doing graduate work at the University of Pennsylvania, so we needed to live in West Philadelphia. You wouldn't believe the places the Realtor showed me. Many were not yet cleaned up from the previous renters. There were dirty dishes in the sink, smelly leftover food in the refrigerator, and piles of trash in the corners. They all could have used a good vacuuming, dusting, and airing. Many of apartments were converted old houses. Some of these apartments only had double- or triple-high bunk beds. I tried to tell the Realtor that I wasn't the typical graduate student, I was newly married. I wanted a decent place to live.

Finally, I found what I thought was the perfect place for us. It was a furnished apartment on the second floor of a three-story attached row house. The house had one apartment on each floor. This apartment had a spacious living room with floor-to-ceiling windows. The room seemed bright and airy. It was directly across the street from Clark Park.

Living across the street from a park was a positive omen for me because I grew up across the street from Prospect Park. Our entrance hallway was large enough to put in a desk and make it into a study. There was a large storage closet in the hall. The bedroom had an antique four-poster bed. I thought that was romantic. There was an oriental rug on the bedroom floor. The room had two decent-sized closets. It was furnished with Victorian furniture, which I loved. The kitchen was square with a tall, built-in pantry and two large windows. A small, round table and three chairs completed the room.

We cleaned the place and then painted the living room, hall, and bedroom. My sister-in-law, Rema, helped us coordinate the neutral color scheme. We bought tie-back drapes and an oval floral rug for the living room. In the bedroom, we hung drapes that matched the new bedspread. Herm polished the wood floors throughout the apartment. The kitchen was too big of a job to tackle as renters. The wallpaper was old, peeling, and faded. The linoleum floor was yellowed and cracked. We intended to live there for only a year until we finished graduate school.

Since the overstuffed chair in the living room was extremely ugly, we decided to get rid of it. We thought about putting it in the basement. Our plans were thwarted when we discovered that the stairs had been altered during the conversion to apartments. It now was so narrow that only one person could travel up or down at a time. There was no way the chair could be transported. So I covered the chair with a decorative spread and pushed it into a corner. It was comfortable and cozy to curl up in and read. Our apartment was fully revamped before the school year began.

The house had belonged to an elderly lady who had recently passed away. She had the house converted to apartments. She lived in this apartment, which occupied the whole second floor. Her daughter was renting it to us. The rent was seventy-five dollars a month. We were within walking distance to school, Herm's work, and everything else we needed. This was city living, which we both were used to.

Next door in the adjoining house lived an Italian couple with two young sons. We quickly became friends. They took us under their wing. We would spend time chatting on the front porch in the evening. They would invite us over for great Italian dinners. We were there when their third son was born.

Our lives were very scheduled. I was in school full time. Herm was on a work-study program. Sunday was clean the house, go to the laundromat, and do the weekly grocery shopping. We did treat ourselves on Sunday evenings by going out to dinner. We had a favorite Italian restaurant where we stuffed ourselves on soup, salad, pasta, and a main course. Dessert was a wonderful rum cake that you could drink off the plate. We always thought that rather funny because Pennsylvania had blue laws, which meant that restaurants weren't allowed to serve liquor or wine on Sundays.

One day Andy, the second son of our neighbors, ran into the street and was hit by a car. For a few days, his life was touch and go, but he turned into a tough little two-year-old. He had multiple fractures throughout his little body. There was the possibility of some brain damage.

Because I was in the second half of my physical therapy program, I offered to work with Anthony in the late afternoons. He was getting weekly PT. At times we included his older brother into our play/therapy sessions. While his legs and arm were in casts, all we could do was gentle range of motion. I really enjoyed my time with these little boys.

PT school was a twelve-month program. The last two months of school were a clinical practice. That meant that I was working but under supervision, like a doctor's internship. Then came graduation. My first paying job was a rehab center where I completed my clinical affiliation.

When our year lease was up, we moved from the city to the suburbs. Herm was still with GE, but he was now working out of the new King of Prussia office. So that's where we moved to. We were one of the first people to move into a brand-new garden apartment complex in King of Prussia called Kingswood Apartments. We rented a first-floor, two-bedroom, two-bath apartment with a patio.

It seemed like a mansion to us, especially because we needed to furnish it. As students, the biggest possessions we owned were books. Herm built a modern bookcase from wood planks and bricks. The first room that we furnished was our bedroom. The bedding, headboard, and frame were new. The dresser, night tables, and lamps were hand-me-downs from our family.

We carpeted the living room, hallway, and master bedroom in neutral tones. Once again, Rema was our decorator. In the eating area off the kitchen, we covered the floor with linoleum. We bought a maple, early-American table with one leaf and four chairs. There was a galley kitchen with all new appliances. This was the first time we had a dishwasher. There were enough cabinets for my two sets of dishes. We wallpapered the small area above the counter and below the cabinets.

Our living room couch was Early American. Above it was a large mirror with two large electric sconces on either side. The second bedroom became a workshop for my husband. There he built a beautiful, large bookcase cabinet that became a room divider for this apartment. The first thing you saw when entering the front door was the kitchen table. But this bookcase blocked the eating area from the living room. The back of it was completely finished because it was open to the eating area. It was an impressive piece of furniture. On either side of the cabinet were matching speakers. This beautiful piece of furniture was finished just in time for us to change the workroom into a nursery.

We became life-long friends with the couple across the hall from us. Unfortunately, they both have passed away. We lived in this apartment for three years. I commuted to work in Philadelphia every day by bus. Luckily, the bus ran in front of our apartment complex. I am a city girl. I am used to sidewalks and public transportation, especially since I can't drive.

In May 1967, we bought a modern, split-level home on Gypsy Lane in King of Prussia. It was a short distance from our apartment. We were the third owner of this ten-year-old home. It was on a wooded, residential street. The house was on a hill with a sloping, tiered backyard. It had four bedrooms, three baths, and an attached, two-car garage. The first floor had an entrance hall, kitchen, and living room/dining room. This hallway had six steps going up to the bedrooms and six steps going down to the rec room. There were three bedrooms and two baths upstairs. Below the main floor was a large rec room with sliding glass doors opening to an outside slate patio. This room also had a door to the garage and six steps down to another bedroom, full bath, and a basement. To us it seemed like a palace.

The family that we purchased the house from had four young children. The only question I asked the mother was, "Did any of your children fall down the backyard hill?" She burst out laughing and then said, "One of the first things they learned was how to lie on their side and roll down the hill. They enjoyed doing that. All their clothes were grass stained." Well that alleviated my fear of the steep backyard. Even I learned how to run up and down both the back and front yards.

I was pregnant with my second child. I took a break from working. We purchased a refrigerator and got telephone service for the house. The kitchen had a built-in booth and table, so we had a place to sit and eat; otherwise the house was empty. I brought what I needed to survive in the house for the day for me and my little daughter, Amy.

Herm would drop me and Amy at the house before he went to work. I needed to clean the house, kosher the kitchen, and plan how to furnish it. The house had no air conditioning. During the summer it was beastly hot. After lunch, Amy and I would take a nap lying on the linoleum floor of the basement bedroom. It was the coolest room in the house.

Some afternoons after our nap I would wheel Amy in her stroller down to the park. There I met some of the other neighborhood mothers and children.

Next, we had room air conditioners installed in the living room and bedrooms. On the weekends, Herm sanded and refinished all the wood floors of the main and upper floors. We painted all the bedrooms and the first floor before we moved in.

Yes, I married a Jewish handyman. I know they are a rarity. Lucky ME! I bless my father-in-law for Herm's skills. In 1913, my father-in-law came to this county from Poland with his sister and mother when he was thirteen. Later in life, he became the super of a six-story, sixty-family apartment building in Bay

Ridge, Brooklyn. He was very skilled and handy at fixing almost anything.

With my decorating ideas and my husband's skill, our house became a comfortable and beautiful warm home. We are still living in it some fifty-four years later. All three of our children were brought up in this house. We all call this place home. My children's hand imprints are in the cement floor of the storage room/ crawl space.

Our apartment living room furniture went into the rec room. It was the center of activity for this home. That is where the console television resided. The living room and dining room remained bare, except for toys, for a number of years.

After twelve years of living in this house, we added a three-floor addition. We more than doubled the size of the rec room. We added a breakfast room off of the kitchen with large windows on two walls overlooking the backyard. This room is always warm, bright, and welcoming. We also added an upstairs laundry room and master bedroom with a sitting room suite. We then painted and redecorated all the children's rooms.

Our builder and crew, who I called Mario and his merry men, were not happy about putting the laundry room on the top floor. I, however, insisted! I insisted because that is where all the laundry comes from. I was tired of going down three flights of steps carrying a heavy, full laundry basket. Also, my husband's workshop was in the basement. When he used a saw, dust got over everything. If I put a pile of clothes on the steps—left (dirty clothes) goes down and right (clean clothes) goes up—the kids just ignored the clothes and stepped over the piles. So the upstairs laundry room was an absolute must-have.

I basically designed the whole addition. I wanted things to be convenient for me. It felt like Mario and his merry men lived with us for about a year. They were great entertainment for my two-year-old son Adam. He would stand at the rec room sliding glass door and just watch them work. I invited Mario and his merry men in to have some birthday cake with Adam when he turned three. They gave Adam a set of plastic tools on a belt just like they wore. The men would display the tool they were using for Adam to see. After that, Adam watched and did whatever he saw them do with his tools. Today Adam, like his paternal grandfather and father, is part of that rare breed, a Jewish handyman.

In the spring of 2001, my husband retired. Adam had finished college and was living at home and working at a local family-owned pizza restaurant. Our daughter Amy also worked there when she was in high school. It was only a few blocks from our house.

Our house project at this time was to upgrade the master bathroom. Herm and Adam were going to do this together. I gave up my dressing room and closet. The new closet was moved to what had been the bedroom sitting area. We still had a spacious bedroom. Adam loved the demolition work of removing floor and wall tiles. Adam had a break at work after lunchtime till before dinner. He and a buddy lugged supplies and heavy boxes of tiles up two flights of steps. They also removed all the trash and smashed tiles.

Before we began work, I informed Herm that we would be moving back into our old bedroom which had become Leah's room. Neither daughter was living at home. Herm couldn't understand why we had to move out. Men! Our bedroom became a dusty storage room while the building was going on. This job took almost two years.

The finished bathroom could be put in a decorating magazine. We included a Jacuzzi bathtub, a glass-enclosed steam room shower, two individual sinks with medicine cabinets, and a vanity table for me.

There were wooden wall storage cabinets and large mirrors above both sinks and vanity.

I used decorative sconces above the bathtub and lighting above the mirrors and in the ceiling. The walls and floor were tiled. Since this was our winter home, we installed heat under the floor tiles and a towel warmer. Herm did all the carpentry, tile, electrical, and plumbing except for moving the waste pipe for the toilet, which Herm hired a professional plumber for. This magnificent bathroom is probably the last major change we will make to this house.

I officially retired in 2012. It became difficult keeping up a PT practice when I would leave Pennsylvania as soon as the weather became cold and not return until the next spring. Now I can say, "I live wherever the weather is like spring and summer."

In 2006, we purchased a home in an active adult community in Florida. Here we spend the fall and winter months. Although I don't like to admit it, Florida is in my blood. My maternal grandparents spent their winters in South Beach, Miami, Florida. My parents lived in Hollywood, and my in-laws lived in Hallandale. During the winter school break, we took our children to visit their grandparents in Florida for two weeks. We all have great memories of those visits.

Moving Forward Leaving Something Behind

The more prepared we are to move forward, the easier it is to leave things behind. For some of us, we are holding on to past identities, others to old clothing, mementos, and trophies, material things that had meaning years ago but not today. Habits that didn't serve us anymore may also be holding us back.

Letting go is a difficult process. However, it is a healthy thing to do; it provides the space for you to continue on your forward path.

Action Exercise

- In how many homes have you lived?
- Which was your favorite house and why?
- Write about a special memory from each home.
- Did you change the house in any way, and if so, why?
- What, if anything, did you leave behind in those homes?
- Draw or paint a picture of your favorite home.

CHAPTER 4

Zora the Collector

Collecting brings joy into my life

I love collecting. I collect friends as well as all manner of things. In fact, the only thing I can think of that I have never collected is husbands! One of the many, many reasons I have stayed married to this man is our belief in the sanctity of marriage vows. I said then—as I say all the time— "...I take this man for better, for worse, and for transportation."

Rusty-Kit

When I was in college living in a girls' dorm, my twin-sized bed hardly had room for me. It was covered with an assortment of stuffed animals. My favorite always sat in a place of honor, high up on my pillows. He was a stuffed Dachshund named Rusty-Kit.

I bought Rusty-Kit one summer when I was a camper at Camp Guilford. A toy manufacturer came to camp that summer and was selling stuffed animals. I fell in love with this dog as soon as I looked into his clear plastic button eyes. He practically jumped into my arms. The dog was fourteen inches long and five inches high. His long, pointed nose and tail were firm. His legs were short and stocky. His ears were floppy with a felt underside. His rusty-looking body, a firm ten-inch circumference, had a smooth, silky fur that felt like velvet.

Since that summer in camp when I was eight, Rusty-Kit has sat on my bed. He came to college with me. He has lived in all my apartments and houses. I have never allowed my children or grandchildren to play with him. From childhood, I have always been extremely possessive of my belongings which I always cared for fastidiously.

I suspect this comes in part from the time when I let a friend keep my new doll overnight. We had been playing, and she begged to sleep with it that night. The next day I came for my doll. Susie went into her room, came out, and handed me the doll's body. Then, she went into another room and returned with the doll's head. I was horrified. I wouldn't touch the decapitated doll.

After that, I avoided this child as much as possible. Since it never occurred to me to speak up for myself, I shared this with no one. So if some child took something of mine, I just assumed it was gone for good. I quickly learned to keep my things very close to me. I have lived ever since with Shakespeare's admonition: "Neither a borrower nor a lender be," with emphasis on the latter.

Rusty-Kit, some sixty-five-plus years later, needs a little surgery. There is a small opening in his stomach seam that needs stitching. The felt lining under his ears has worn away and needs to be replaced. His snout has lost its stuffing, and it is collapsed in on itself. However, his eyes are still the bright, clear, round plastic buttons I fell in love with when I was a child.

When I bought him, I gave him the name Rusty because that was how he looked to me. It also sounded like a dog's name. He became my pet. Living in an apartment in Brooklyn, goldfish from the Five and Dime and guppies scooped from the lake in Prospect Park had been my only live pets.

When I was thirteen and a CIT, counselor in training, at Camp Che Na Wah, my bunkmates and I had a crush on a much older counselor at the brother camp. His nickname was Kit.

That year Rusty's name became Rusty-Kit. The name has stuck. Rusty-Kit was with me in my pre-diary writing days. We would communicate through mental telepathy. He knew my thoughts and secrets as I would think them. Rusty-Kit assured me he would always be with me as long as I needed him, but I shouldn't count on Kit. In that matter Rusty-Kit was absolutely correct.

Rusty-Kit is my oldest self-bought personal possession. This purchase began a life-long process of collecting things that interested or intrigued me. He now guards my large collection of character telephones on display in my girls' bedroom. Rusty-Kit stands on a high fluffy pillow surrounded by other stuffed animals that my daughters left behind.

Ricky the Raccoon

The twin beds in my girls' room have stuffed teddy bears, dogs, and a hairy raccoon puppet. Ricky the Raccoon was a puppet I used in my therapy practice to communicate with children. Most children would talk more freely and easily to a puppet than to an adult.

They loved petting his fluffy tail and having his soft fur brush against their arms and legs.

Tactile sensory stimulation is also a form of therapy that involves the sensation of touch and texture. It is a therapy often used with autistic children, stroke patients and adults with dementia. Therapists also work with tactile-sensitive individuals to desensitize them.

When I retired, I brought Ricky upstairs to the girls' room to be with other animal friends. A few summers ago, I gave Ricky the Raccoon to my long-time friend. She and her husband have a summer cottage in the woods on a lake in the Adirondacks, Upstate New York not far from Camp Che Na Wah. This friend had a collection of stuffed woodland animals sitting on her living room couch. I just knew Ricky the Raccoon would feel at home there, rather than living in the suburbs. I usually visit Ricky the Raccoon along with my human friends during the summer.

Diaries

In my early teens, I began keeping an actual diary. I wrote in old, unfinished school notebooks because I was sure nobody would look in them and discover my secrets. Then my father gave me a six-by-nine-inch lined, hard-covered diary in 1953. It was set up to be used as either an appointment book or journal. On the top of each page were the day, month, and year. Each year the cover was a different color. Dad got these for his dental office and never used them, so he gave them to me. One page a day was just enough to get me started journaling.

I was thirteen when I started keeping a diary, the same age as Anne Frank. For her thirteenth birthday, June 12, 1942, Anne's father presented her with a red-and-white checkered notebook for her to use as a diary. She began writing in it immediately, which ended up being shortly before she and her family went into hiding from the Nazis. For the next two years and thirty-five days, she recorded her activities, thoughts, and feelings in this notebook. The discovery and publication of this diary after the war and her early death have been of enormous value in providing the public with an unvarnished view of life in Europe during Hitler's reign of terror.

For the last twenty years, I have been writing in large, hard-covered, eight-by-ten-inch sketchbooks. Journals have lines, sketchbooks have blank pages. I prefer blank pages. I am a lefty. My handwriting usually is on a slant. I don't like being confined by lines or confined by anything. Some days my writing is large and loopy. Other days it is tight and cramped causing it to be almost impossible to read. As my feelings change so does my handwriting. When I am angry, I tend to press heavily. If I had a crush on a guy, his name was surrounded by a heart and was written with very carefully formed pen strokes. Sometimes I doodled at the edge of a page.

My personal journal collection takes up at least two long, tightly packed bookshelves. Though the journals are all the same size, the covers from each year differ in color and design. What will my children do with twenty years of my journals? Probably just toss them. Or maybe they will read them to see what I had to say about *them*. Or maybe I will toss them myself someday after this book is published as a *New York Times* bestseller. I believe if you are going to dream, DREAM BIG!

I have been told by other collectors that one item is a novelty, two are a pair, and three are the start of a collection. I agree wholeheartedly with this assessment. I have many collections.

I'm not certain how I became hooked on this passion. Perhaps it is genetic.

My parents collected antiques. My mom and I loved browsing flea markets and thrift shops up north in

Pennsylvania, I have two friends that love going to thrift shops, and we usually make a day of it. Of course, we also do lunch. I often find something that I really don't need but couldn't live without because it was such a bargain. I am however, getting ahead of myself.

Avon Bottles

As an adult, the very first thing I collected was Avon bottles. A friend of mine was an Avon sales representative. Avon is a company that started in 1886. They sold cosmetics, fragrances, and other beauty products in whimsical and decorative glass bottles such as cars, telephones, heads of famous people, animals, and a variety of other things. They are still in business today. Their advertising jingle was "Avon Calling" because they sold door-to-door or had house parties. Door-to-door selling reminds me of the Fuller Brush man. Now that's a blast from my childhood.

The first Avon bottles that I purchased were glass vintage car models. They came in a variety of colors (blue, green, gray, and amber) filled with aftershave lotion. Herm and I both liked the fragrance. He received them from me as gifts for his birthday, anniversary, Chanukah, or because he ran out. As the bottles became empty, I lined them up on the dining room windowsill for decoration.

The number of cars and variety of vehicle styles quickly increased. Some of the cars I owned included a '64 Mustang, a station wagon, a Thunderbird, a Ferrari, a '55 Chevy, a Chrysler, and a Rolls Royce. Herm dreamed of owning a Rolls Royce. Having this aftershave bottle was the closest he got to having one. Our actual car was a Dodge station wagon—a bit more practical to cart around our young family.

Later on (perhaps anticipating my largest and most pervasive collection), I purchased every style of telephone Avon made: candlestick, wall, desk model, and French cradle phone. These were filled with either men or women's cologne. These empty telephone bottles are now displayed in my bathrooms.

I eventually sold off the car collection when I ran out of windowsill space. I replaced the glass Avon cars with antique glass candy containers. My first two purchases were an iron and a doll's baby bottle. These glass candy containers filled with colorful sugar pellets remind me of my paternal grandmother. Almost every time she visited us she would first stop at Woolworth's Five & Dime and buy my brother and me an appropriate style glass candy container. Once we devoured the yummy candies, we had a new toy to play with. It was amazing how sturdy these glass toys were. We never broke one.

This grandma used to play card games—Casino and Steal the Old Man's Bundle—with me. These games challenged my matching and addition skills. Grandma always let me win, which made me feel good. Grandma was old, thin, and stood erect. She always seemed frail and fragile to me. She died before I got to know her as well as I would have liked.

I remember one Sunday morning my aunts and uncles coming to our house to pick up my parents. They often went out to lunch together. This particular day they were going to my Grandma Isaacs's funeral. I hadn't been told that she had died. So as they all left, I said, "Have a good time." How could I have been so clueless and insensitive?

It is now many years later and this still upsets me. In fact, tears are forming in the corner of my eyes as I write this. Not telling children bad news was another way of keeping family secrets.

Grandma's legacy is my continued interest in collecting glass items. The first produced glass candy containers were in the shape of Independence Hall and the Liberty Bell. I own a Liberty Bell. They were manufactured at the time of the Centennial Exposition in 1876. By 1900, these candy containers were being mass-produced. The four major manufacturers were in

Pennsylvania. During the pre-Depression time, 1900–1920, the container seals were metal. In the 1940s, after the Great Depression when metal was scarce, the seals became cardboard, cork, or wood.

Today most old candy containers are found without seals. If they are sealed with the candy still inside, they sell for a higher price. I have a number of filled and sealed candy containers. Like Avon bottles, candy containers came in many styles: trains, cars, boats, animals, lanterns, telephones, and holiday items to name a few.

My candy containers cover three knick-knack shelves on my dining room paneled wall. Next to my prized baby bottle, iron, and Liberty Bell, I have animals, trains, cars, lanterns, and luggage. In addition, telephone items are located all through the house wherever I could find an empty space on a shelf. My candy container collection has remained rather small because I became an *uber* antique-telephone collector.

Telephones

Let me tell you about my largest collection. It all began one day as I was reading a *Woman's Day* magazine in the early 1960s. An ad at the back of the magazine caught my eye. Canada was updating their equipment from operator telephones to rotary dial phones and was selling Western Electric wooden wall phones in working condition. This phone had brass bells on the top front, a speaker arm in the front middle, a separate receiver on one side, and a crank that rang the bells on the opposite side.

For some unknown reason at that time, I had to have that phone. It cost more than two weeks' worth of groceries for my husband and me. Even so, I bought it. The wall phone arrived well packed and in perfect condition. I loved it then and love it still!

We hung it in a place of honor outside the kitchen in the eating area of our King of Prussia apartment. Its profile could be seen by anyone who entered. It certainly was a conversation piece! (Pun intended.) My husband hooked it up as an extension phone. We couldn't make calls from it, but we could use it to both listen and speak. That way Herm and I could be on the same phone call together. It was our unique way of having an extension. Our guests loved to turn the crank and make the melodious shiny brass bells ring.

Shortly after that acquisition, Mom and I went to the Collegeville Antique/Flea Market; I came home with two old candlestick telephones. These are also known as Eliot Ness phones. My phone collection started. I know that because I owned three antique telephones. As I previously mentioned: one is a novelty, two is a pair, and three is the beginning of a collection.

One of the guys I bought phones from, a collector himself, told me about an international telephone club. Of course, I immediately became a member. I was member #333 of the Antique Telephone Collectors Association (ATCA). Intuitively, I believe triple three is a magic number. According to numerology, the number three stands for abundance and happy communication. Need I say more? I just sensed that collecting telephones was going to be a fun and exciting hobby. And now more than fifty years later, I know this to be true.

I received monthly ATCA newsletters with informative articles, listings of telephone shows, and items that collectors were selling. Soon a second international telephone club was established—Telephone Collectors International (TCI). So, I joined that club as well. The next thing I knew I was asked to find a place to hold a TCI show in Pennsylvania. It was not long before I was running the TCI telephone show in Radnor, PA with the help of my two guy telephone pals.

Unbeknownst to us, the hotel where we were holding the show changed owners as well as its name on the very Friday that our TCI show was scheduled to begin. You can imagine the confusion this caused. Even with all of the resulting chaos, the show was a great success. The next year, we moved the show to Wilmington, Delaware, and then the year after to Lancaster, PA. This annual fall TCI antique telephone show has remained in Lancaster since then.

Although my son, Adam, helped set up the shows, neither he nor his sisters have ever been impressed with my phone collection. Their friends, however, seemed to be. They often asked if they could use the unusual phones to make calls. As my collection has grown, my friends sometimes comment that my house seems like a museum. Maybe, I should charge admission?

I have given talks on the history of the telephone to the Sisterhood of my synagogue and a few other local groups. My collection was written up in the *King of Prussia Courier* many years ago. Recently an article about my telephone collecting was printed in the 2017 summer issue of *The Grapevine*, our Florida community's magazine.

As one might imagine, antique telephone collecting is mainly a male hobby. Many of the collectors have worked for Ma Bell or other phone companies. Legend has it that some enterprising collectors, while working for these phone companies, would go into small-town, old candy or drug stores and present the owners with new phone signs to replace the antique ones. This ruse allowed the collector to significantly enhance their personal sign collection, while making the small-town store owners proud of their more modern advertising. Thus, the entrepreneurs were able to rationalize they had created a win-win situation.

My phone collection is eclectic. I have multiples of nearly all phone styles: wooden and metal wall phones, candlestick, coin box, rotary dial, vanity, princess, trim line, police, firebox, and telephones from other countries. Also included are novelty and character phones featuring Mickey, Minnie Mouse, Snoopy, and Superman. Phone signs, advertisements, ceramic and glass insulators, jewelry, greeting cards, and postcards are also a part of my vast collection of telephone paraphernalia.

A few of Zora's many antique telephones.

Toy phones, phone coffee mugs, teapots, cookie jars, drinking glasses, ashtrays, Avon bottles, pillows, gossip benches, and phone tables round out my collection. I even have items of clothing with phones on them which I proudly wear.

My personal favorite phone is a black patent-leather shoulder-strap pocketbook that is a push-button telephone with a receiver and phone jack to plug it in. I could plug it in at anyone's house and make a phone call. The call would be on their bill!

The pocketbook phone mechanism was inside the bag, thus there was little room for more than a wallet, hankie, comb, and lipstick. When I use this pocketbook, it generally creates conversation. I especially enjoy wearing it to telephone shows. This phone can be seen in the Amsterdam Museum of Bags and Purses. I was delightedly surprised to find an exact copy of my pocketbook on display when I visited this museum in April 2011.

Phone Connections

I believe in keeping secrets. Call it superstition if you want. I never announce my pregnancies until it is physically obvious. When I informed my thirteen- and ten-year-old daughters about my next pregnancy, I told them it was a secret, and I would let them know when they could tell people. The day I gave then permission to tell was a Hebrew School afternoon. My dear friend Ann had Hebrew School carpool home.

My younger daughter, Leah, told Ann that I was pregnant. Ann sternly told Leah not to make up such stories about her mother. Leah came home in tears. Blubbering, "Mrs. S. said I shouldn't tell such stories about you." A few minutes later the phone rang. I didn't say hello or ask who was calling (This was way before caller ID.). I just said cheerfully, "Yes, it is true!"

Ann and I had been good friends for many years. We met at a synagogue picnic when we were both pregnant, I with my second child, Leah, and she with her third child. Our two younger daughters became friends as did our older girls. They all went to school together from kindergarten through high school. Ann and I were our daughters' Brownie and Girl Scout leaders. She still lives in the neighborhood and our friendship continues.

Ann and I did have one unusual misunderstanding. She tried to reach me by telephone a number of times, and my line was dead. Thinking she was doing me a favor, she called the phone company to have them correct whatever was wrong. Those were the days when all phones were bought from Ma Bell and you paid for each extension phone. I had a different color rotary dial phone hooked up in each room of my home.

I had already started my antique telephone collection. I had more extensions than were officially listed with the phone company, and I had enough phones to change the extensions on a daily basis if I had wished too.

I was unaware that my phones weren't working. So when a phone truck parked at the top of the driveway and a repairman came to the door unexpectedly, I was in a state of panic. Could they throw me in jail for all my contraband?

He rang the doorbell and told me that a neighbor reported my phone out of order. I told him to check the lines outside, and that I can't let him in because I am alone. He returned and rang the bell again to say he needed to check a connection in the garage. As I opened the garage door for him, I was standing in the house door that leads to my rec room. In this room there are phones of all vintages on the walls and tables. I even have a 1940s candy store wooden phone booth with a vintage payphone in it.

The man's eyes popped open. He asked if he could see my collection. "Only if you promised not to report me to the phone company," I told him. He was fascinated with my collection and knowledge of telephones. He did say that I didn't need to worry about Ma Bell coming after me.

As it turned out, he was able to fix the problem with my phone system by playing with the wires in the garage. He even let me take a photo of him in his phone truck at the top of my driveway.

As soon as he left, I called my friend Ann and told her never to call the phone company without telling me first!

Jim Beam Bottles

In 1979, Jim Beam produced a collection of glass whiskey bottles in antique telephone styles. Yes, I have almost all of them. Some of these bottles are full and still unopened. Many are in their original cardboard cartons. Unfortunately, to mail them for sale, they must be empty. So what do you think, should I start drinking?

One of my favorite acquisitions is a 1940s wooden phone booth with glass bifold doors. The booth light and fan go on as the bifold door is closed. You may, if you are of a certain age, remember these phone booths from candy and drug stores.

I also possess an early switchboard with cloth connection plugs. You may recall seeing this style switchboard on TV when Lily Tomlin played Ernestine, a comic telephone operator saying, "Number, please" in a heavily nasal Brooklyn accent.

Handy Herman hooked up a number of rotary dial telephones to this switchboard. My children loved mimicking Ernestine as they played switchboard operator, making the various phones around the house ring. The girls' Brooklyn accents were especially good considering both their parents were born and bred in Brooklyn.

Telephone Books

No longer does the phone company leave at your door thick, heavy phone books which alphabetically listed everybody's phone number and address in town. I have a few bookshelves reserved for reference books about telephones. These shelves also contain an assortment of children's books about phones. In one picture book, there is a description of the proper etiquette for answering the telephone. The polite way to answer the telephone was: "Hello, this is the Natanblut residence, Zora speaking. To whom do you wish to speak?" When was the last time you heard that greeting coming from the other end of the receiver?

Cell phones and home phones now announce who is calling both audibly and visually. I also have a children's book about phones written in Hebrew which I bought in Israel. Once upon a time, a long time ago, I could read and translate that entire short book.

All three of my children, like many of their contemporaries, don't have telephone land lines in their homes; they rely exclusively on their cell phones.

As a child, I enjoyed the make-believe world of the comic-strip detective Dick Tracy with his two-way wristwatch radio. It was clearly science fiction then. Now wristwatches are mini computers that talk to you, record how many steps you take in a day, receive and send text messages. They even show email messages. Today, it is becoming rare for cell phone users to even remember rotary dial, pay phones, or phone booths.

Many walls are covered floor to ceiling with telephones, and so are the tables in my house. As my children grew up and left home, I emptied their rooms of their books and belongings so that I could use their walls and bookcases to expand my phone display. Even the bathrooms have old phones in them. My friends are indeed correct. I do have a virtual museum in my house. I will admit that my house is a duster's nightmare. Thank goodness for cleaning help.

A fun "phone-y" thing I used to do when I had a new babysitter was to say as I was leaving the house, "If the phone rings, just answer it." We left before I would bother to mention which phone was actually hooked up.

In analyzing my fascination with phones, I have asked myself, "What do telephones say about me?" As a child and young adult, I didn't want to be seen by teachers or adults. A telephone let me communicate "sight unseen." My grasp on the receiver gave me a sense of stability and even strength. It was something cylindrical, solid and smooth for my hand to grasp. This made me feel that I was in control and had the option to speak or disconnect.

As a child, the telephone was always special to me. I enjoyed both making and receiving calls. It was fun to spin the dial and then watch it rotate as I counted the clicks of the dialed number. I also enjoyed the sound of a ringing phone. I thought of it as a pleasant musical interruption.

Growing up, a phone call for me usually meant an invitation for a playdate. As I grew older, it was a chat with a girlfriend. "What should we wear to school tomorrow?" "Have you seen that new cute boy at school?" A call from a boy was the best kind of phone call. "Sure, I'd love to go to the movies Saturday night." Occasionally I had to answer my father's dental office phone. Then I acted very grown up and professional. "Dr. Isaacs's office, may I take a message?"

Party Line

When we first lived in Pennsylvania, our telephone was a less-expensive party line. We chose this option because we knew nobody there. For my younger readers, a party line was an option for multiple telephone customers to use the same equipment even though they had individual phone numbers. I enjoyed occasionally eavesdropping on the phone. I never wondered if they listened to our phone calls to our parents, siblings, and friends. The only people we chatted with were in Brooklyn.

Our move to Philadelphia was over fifty-five years ago. I can't believe in that time how many things have become obsolete. I, of course, have been most aware of the changes in communication; principally, the telephone. The changes in my lifetime have been phenomenal.

When my mother was in her eighties, I asked her what had been the biggest change during her lifetime.

So much history happened considering she grew up during the Industrial Revolution. She immediately replied, "A man on the moon, and I could see him for myself on TV." Up until that time, Mom believed that was something that only could have happened in a Jules Verne novel.

My focus seems to have always been on communication. I attribute that to the profound influence of reading about Dick Tracy and his two-way radio wristwatch. So here I am now with my historical telephone relics which are requiring me to stay in my original home even though we no longer need such a spacious place for just the two of us. My possessions now own me! Who else might be interested in so many artifacts of the previous century? Everybody, young and old, is clamoring for the newest iPad and cell phone. I seem very much out of step continuing to work on preserving the past.

I am clearly carrying on the tradition of my parents by collecting antiques. Mine are just a different kind. Other people might think that my collecting spirit is a tad over the top. Evidently, I didn't pass this spirit on to my children. However, my youngest granddaughter, Melanie, is following in the family tradition of collecting but with a twist. She seeks out certain items and then gifts them to me.

My Hippo Collection

When little Melanie heard that I was a hippotherapist, she laughed thinking that I treated hippopotamuses. So Melanie started collecting stuffed, ceramic, stone, and plastic hippos whenever she could find them. She then presented them to me. I kept this collection in my physical therapy office on the windowsill. It always amused my clients and me.

While the client is sitting upon the horse's back, the horse's gait rhythmically moves the client's trunk and pelvis. Thus, the client's muscles are alternatively tensed and relaxed. Hippotherapy also gives the client a chance to be out in the fresh air and see the world from a higher vantage point. Many clients consider this activity more fun and recreational than indoor therapy.

Hands and Hamsas

Since I am a manual physical therapist, my hands are the primary tools of my trade. I started to collect interesting hands wherever I found them. It is amazing how many positions and expressions a human hand can form. The hands I collect are all sizes made in different countries and from different materials such as wood, terra cotta, ceramic, plastic, glass, and metal. Added to this is my Hamsa collection, another type of hand.

A Hamsa is a Middle Eastern good luck charm used to ward off the evil eye and is worn by people of differing religions around the world. The evil eye has been perceived as a malevolent gaze intended to inflict harm, suffering, illness, or bad luck.

Hamsa means five and refers to the fingers. It is a hand-shaped talisman with three straight fingers together in the middle with thumbs on both sides. Many have decorations in the center of the palm. Jews refer to the Hamsa as the hand of God or the hand of Miriam. Muslims call it the hand of Fatima.

The Hamsa goes back to the classic Greek and Roman period. It is found on almost every continent. It is mentioned in the Jewish text, *Ethics of Our Fathers*. In Hebrew, we say, *"b' li' ayah hara"*—without the evil eye. In Yiddish, the phrase is *"Keyn ayn horeh."* It means not to be bewitched by looking at. Ashkenazi (Eastern European) Jews have believed that excess praise causes vulnerability from the evil eye.

A particular treasure I found upon opening a velour box while strolling through a thrift shop was a pair of terra cotta Indian *mudra* prayer hands. Each hand holds a tea light candle. The left hand's thumb touches the forefingers with the palm facing upward, a gesture symbolizing wisdom. The right hand is also facing up with the tip of the thumb and first finger touching each other. This gesture symbolizes hope. Together, the two hands holding tea lights convey the following benediction: "May wisdom guide you and hope sustain you." I certainly could not leave them there for someone else to buy. They now reside in my Pennsylvania home next to my Sabbath candles.

My collection of hands symbolizes my profession as a manual or hands-on physical therapist. It is no coincidence that I chose this profession because I think of myself as a very tactile person. Hands perform an infinite number of tasks and functions. Because of their dexterity and flexibility, hands not only enable us to accomplish complex tasks, but they can also fill in for our other senses. Hands for the deaf express their speech. Hands can express direction, prayer, movement, friendship and emotions. And at times I use my hands to feel fine details that my eyes don't pick up.

The versatility of hands can be discovered in how we use the word. I like to give my clients a guiding hand; I enjoy walking hand-in-hand with my grandchildren. In an argument I want the upper hand!

Other common idioms illustrate the multiple ways in which we think of hands. Some of these are reflected in expressions such as: I'm an old hand at doing that; I know it like the back of my hand; you're playing into his hand; don't be underhanded; let's have a show of hands; and all hands on deck. Now, I am ready to wash my hands of this *handy* list.

Angels

In addition to my array of hands in my Florida home, I have expanded my collections to include angels, mermaids, dolphins, and fairies. They reflect my interest in spirituality, prayer, and healing. The belief surrounding them is they confer blessings and good fortune from the three biospheres: sky, land, and water. My first introduction to angels was as a child listening to the opera *Hansel and Gretel* by Engelbert Humperdinck on the big console radio in our living room.

On many Saturday afternoons, Mom and I would listen to Milton Cross explain the opera that would be broadcast live from the Metropolitan Opera House in New York City. Milton Cross would always begin his program by saying, "Good afternoon, opera lovers from coast to coast." He would explain the plot and then introduce the cast during the intermission.

Before the show began, Mom would play some of the opera's main musical themes for me on our baby grand piano. That was the only time I remember the piano being played.

Wait! That's not true. For a very short time I was given a few piano lessons. The music wasn't written large enough for me to read while seated on the piano bench. Standing, I could get close enough to read the music, but my arms weren't in a proper position for my hands to reach the keyboard. Consequently, my musical career was understandably short lived.

In the story, Hansel and Gretel are lost in the woods. It is late at night. Before they drift off, they sing a prayer asking fourteen angels to guard them while they sleep. After a safe night's slumber, the dew fairies wake them. The music sounded so beautiful and moving, I could visualize what was happening. From my exposure to Christmas pageants in elementary school, I was aware that Christians believe in angels. I even was chosen to be an angel in the pageant.

Later on, when I became well-versed in Judaism, I learned that angels are very much a part of our religion. The Hebrew word for angel is *malakh*. It is the Jewish belief that angels have been the link between God and man. They function as our protector, helper, and messenger from God.

Angels have been described as metaphysical beings with no free will or physical body. Angels teach, comfort, and explain. It was an angel who informed Abraham and Sarah that they would have a child even though they were an exceedingly elderly couple. It was another angel who stopped Abraham from sacrificing Isaac. And in the story of Jacob's dream, he wrestles with an angel on a ladder. These are but a few of the biblical stories in which God directs his angels to intervene to protect or help those in need.

As a child, it was easy for me to believe in angels and I still do. Three sculpted angels are seated on the entrance gate of the private courtyard in front of our house welcoming guests to my home in Florida.

Yes, in our foyer is my favorite angel resting in a hand, thus combining two of my collections, angels and hands. The hand is positioned to look like a comfortable upholstered chair. Resting in the palm of the right hand is the angel's head and torso facing the thumb. The fingers are close together and pointing upward like the back of a chair. The palm is the cushioned seat. The wrist is bent backwards and acts as the chair's support.

The angel's wings are spread across its back with a lovely white rose surrounded by green leaves between the wings. The angel's body is bent over the palm, and its legs are draped downward next to the wrist. It is made of white plaster of Paris and is sprinkled with silver glitter, "fairy" dust. The angel's body position reminds me of my children when they were little.

With their feet on the floor they would fold themselves over the seat of the couch resting quietly for a few moments. It made me believe they were giving themselves a personal time out.

Zebras

In recent years, I have also started a small collection of zebras. I began with five, and I promised myself I would not get any more zebras than would fit on the small cabinet shelf they occupy. But this self-promise has not stopped my children and friends from getting me additional zebra knickknacks. Many of my zebras are utilitarian: a coffee mug; a planter; napkin rings; salt and pepper shakers; a small, rectangular ceramic tray; a paperweight; and a tall, ceremonial rattle.

My prized and probably most expensive zebra is a brand-new whistling teakettle. I keep it on display rather than use it in the kitchen. That my zebra count is now up to over fifteen and has expanded onto a second shelf probably won't sound like a big surprise to any of my readers.

I also express my zebra passion by the clothes I wear, which are usually bold black-and-white stripes. I also own many zebra accessories to enhance my non-zebra clothing: jackets, sweaters, hats, scarves, pocketbooks, shoes, sneakers, and a large assortment of zebra jewelry.

I believe that the zebra is my spirit or totem animal because we share a black-and-white world. I see only black and white. A zebra's body is black skin under a white hairy coat. It's noteworthy that each zebra has its own unique pattern of stripes. Its strengths are beauty, balance, and grace. These are qualities I aspire to have. Maria Tallchief, a ballet dancer; Sonja Henie, a figure skater; and Esther Williams, the famed Hollywood swimmer, exhibit these qualities.

Zebra's stripes are similar to human's finger prints. It is a form of identity. A zebra foal recognizes its mother by her skin pattern, smell, and voice. A most interesting notion to me is that some scientists believe that zebras see colors. I wish I did.

Other traits we share are our tranquility and non-aggressive natures. On a purely serendipitous level, both Zora and Zebra begin with a Z and end with an R and A.

Just like many other people, I find comfort being surrounded by family and friends. When zebras stand together as a herd, they are providing safety for each other. They confuse and dazzle their predators with all the stripes. It is impossible for a lion to discern where one individual animal ends and another begins. As long as they remain a unit, their safety is enhanced. Similar to the zebra, I feel supported, sustained, and protected by family and my extended community.

Safaris travel in a similar grouping. Passengers in open Jeeps are instructed to remain still and not stand up so that the large presence of the vehicle appears too formidable for a lion or other large predator to consider attacking.

Some scientists believe that the stripes also protect zebras from the heat of the blazing sun as well as insect bites. Zebras can gallop about forty miles per hour. When being chased, they tend to use a zigzag pattern to escape. They can usually outrun their predators. When provoked, their tranquility dissolves and they become fierce fighters using their sharp teeth and hooves. They will encircle and protect an injured member.

Zebras are part of the Equus family along with horses and donkeys. All these animals sleep standing up. They make similar whinnying sounds like horses to alert others of danger. They are herbivorous and have a life span of about twenty-five years. They are social animals that live in harems of about six females to one male. Unlike the horse, they strongly resist being domesticated.

I am sure this is more trivia than most people care about. But I found it fascinating. Who knows, maybe someday my husband's favorite TV quiz show, *Jeopardy*, may have a zebra question and you'll be able to respond correctly. If so, please tell emcee, Alex Trebek, that you learned the answer here in my memoir, *Who Is Zora? Sight Unseen.*

While looking up the characteristics of a zebra, another black-and-white striped animal caught my attention because of its name: the zorilla. It is a member of the skunk family that lives in Africa. My name is part of its name **ZOR**ill**A**. It is also black with a white streak down its back. Like a skunk, the zorilla emits a strong-smelling liquid from its anal glands when threatened. Its scent is less pungent than a skunk's. Zorillas are gentle, shy and peace loving. They rarely, if ever, initiate aggression, which perhaps is one of the reasons they have few enemies. I never heard of this animal before and therefore had to add this piece of trivia. So now you know it too.

Zorillas, as part of the skunk family, bring to mind a cute family vacation story. We were at a camp site in western Pennsylvania. Herm and I were setting up our small canvas, floorless tent on a woodsy site. Other larger and more upscale tents were in view. Our three-year old daughter, Amy, was playing nearby.

The sun was going down, so it was time to start a fire to cook dinner. Amy and I needed to find some kindling to start the campfire. We cooked all our meals over an open flame. Looking up, I heard my cute, blonde little daughter calling in her childish voice "Come here, puddy tat!" She was trailing a small, round black animal with a broad white stripe down its back and tail.

I quickly stood up and called out in a loud voice, "Amy, come here for a cookie." To Amy a cookie was better than a "puddy tat." Luckily, she still smelled like a sweet little girl.

Antiques

My home in Pennsylvania is furnished with much antique furniture. One of our first purchases was a petite antique Victorian loveseat. When we brought it home, the horsehair stuffing was sticking out through the frayed and faded damask fabric. The delicate wooden frame desperately needed to be refinished. But in my mind's eye, I could see its potential beauty.

My father-in-law, who couldn't foresee the loveseat's charm, thought out loud, "What a waste of money."

However, after Herman stripped and refinished the wooden frame, I sent it out to be completely cleaned, structurally tightened up and reupholstered with a rich-looking red-floral velour fabric. When it came back, it was hard for my father-in-law to believe his eyes. He gentlemanly apologized for his previous thought and words. Victorian and red became and remain the theme for the first floor of our modern split-level home.

My best antique furniture bargain was a mirrored wooden oak icebox from a flea market. I got it for five dollars! It was in perfect condition and didn't need any refinishing whatsoever. Next to it in the breakfast room, where it now resides, stands a tall, wide, oak Hoosier, also known as a kitchen work station.

Behind the first of the top three hinged wooden doors of the Hoosier is a metal flour sifter. On the back of these doors are metal spice racks filled with empty antique metal spice cans which once contained cinnamon and other baking condiments. The inside shelf provides space for storage. Below this area are tambour doors that roll up, revealing more storage space and a pull-out porcelain countertop for rolling cookie and pie dough.

Supporting this work surface is a large storage area with another pull-out shelf on one side. Three drawers of increasing size from top to bottom fill the other side. The lowest and largest drawer is a metal-lined bread drawer. This huge baking station stands on stubby-but-sturdy wooden legs.

I could not pass this Hoosier up because it reminded me of the one in my grandma Erna's apartment, though she only had the bottom half. It was here where together we rolled our pie and cookie dough. I always found it amusing that Grandma did her own baking even though Grandpa owned the best kosher bakery in Brooklyn.

While collecting may seem like a frivolous activity, I have derived a great deal of benefit from this practice. I find that when I pursue a particular passion amassing unique items relating to my interests, my soul feels nourished and joyful. I feel that I have accomplished something special by saving a piece of the past. It leads me to do research. Collecting makes shopping seem like an adventure for me. I never know where or when I will find the next unusual, unique, or antique item that will enhance one of my collections. I can look at tangible objects and see how they will express or reflect various aspects of myself.

Moreover, collecting has brought me some of the personal recognition and acknowledgement in adulthood that I missed as a young person. As a result of the negativity I experienced at the unkind words of classmates and neighborhood children, my self-worth was seriously diminished. My attempts to remain invisible also caused my teachers to often just ignore me. And, as long as I was unseen and quiet, I didn't create any complications or problems for them. Most likely they had no idea how to help me.

Being recognized for the uniqueness I demonstrate, in part because of my collections, has helped to enhance my happiness, contentment, and my self-esteem. I aspire to be more like the zebra blending into the crowd without losing my individuality.

For me collecting has become habit forming. I admit to being a creature of habit, and I learn best through constant repetition. The more familiar I am with doing something, the more sense of enjoyment I receive from it. Collecting and preserving the past must be a gene my parents passed on to me. From childhood I have learned to value and take care of my possessions. My collections help to define me and tell the story of my interests. They are a large, tangible piece of my legacy.

Collecting

I have found that collections seem to start you, not the other way around. You either are or are not a collector.

A collector is someone who accumulates things. They usually have trouble throwing things away.

One item is a novelty.

Two items are a pair.

Three items are the start of a collection.

Action Exercise

1. A thing comes into your possession because it looks good, it's interesting, amusing, historic, or it reminds you of something your grandparents or parents had. The item is special to you even if you can't explain why.
2. Acquiring: purchase, gift, a find on trash day
3. Upgrading: want an item in better condition, older, more unusual.
4. Quality is more important than quantity.
5. Collect for pleasure not investment. The thrill of the hunt is the happiness of a new find.
6. Buy in person: feel, inspect, and bargain for a lower price.
7. Keep records: description of item, where/when purchased, price.
8. Research items: date, manufacturer, previous owner, unusual details.
9. Join a club of people who collect what you collect.
10. Display items on walls, bookcases, tables, cupboards.

I'd love to hear about your collection. You can contact me at zorapt@email.com

CHAPTER 5

Crafty Me

I have the ability to create anything I want.

After a fun-filled evening of making macramé monkeys hanging from a tree branch, I went upstairs to take an aromatic bubble bath before going to bed. The oval tub was angled in the left-hand corner of the bathroom. Directly above the tub was a rectangular window in the ceiling. When reclining in the tub, I had a beautiful view of the night sky filled with twinkling stars.

My bare feet were aware of the change in sensation as I stepped from the soft, fluffy carpet onto the cold, hard surface of the bathroom's tile floor. I approached the tub and gingerly tested the water with my right foot before climbing into it. I sank below the rose-scented bubbles, my head resting on an inflated plastic pillow. This was my time to reflect, relax, and unwind from the day's hustle and bustle.

Crafts by Mail

As a mother of young children, my evenings became enjoyable when I discovered *The Craft of the Month Club* in an ad at the back of a *Women's Day* magazine. For a nominal fee, I would receive a monthly mailed package that contained everything needed to complete a craft item. Each ingredient was clearly labeled and carefully packaged. There was always a beautiful picture postcard of the finished project, detailed instructions with step-by-step pictures of how to proceed. All the materials that were needed to complete the craft were included, even glue, paints, and brushes. The paints were labeled by color.

The items varied every month. There were fabric items to embroider or crewel, toile items to paint, ceramic items to bake in the oven and paint. These items were practical and could be used as gifts or home decorations. Some of the items I made were aprons, napkin or letter holders, picture frames, trinket boxes, coasters, ashtrays, and origami. There were many knitted, crocheted, crewel, embroidered, and woven articles.

My favorite useful item that I assembled and decorated with a painted floral design was a small metal dustpan and a wooden whisk broom. I used it to sweep crumbs off the table. It is still being used many decades later.

Each month I eagerly anticipated my craft package. Opening the box presented a surprise, a challenge, and an activity to keep me busy at night.

Next, I became nuts for knotting, creating macramé animal wall hangings and planters. Macramé items were all the rage at that time. Once I made the macramé planters, they needed to be filled. So, the next things I made were fabric flowers, some out of burlap, others from chiffon. Then I arranged the bouquets in the planters.

As I created my crafts on the kitchen table, I could hear the shouts from the TV downstairs where my husband was watching sports. Upstairs my children were snug in their beds.

Crocheting and Knitting

Crocheting was an activity I could do while traveling in the car, listening to a lecture, or watching TV.

Crocheting *kippah*, skull caps, became my next endeavor. I crocheted them for my son's Bris (circumcision), Bar/Bat Mitzvahs, and weddings. Each of my children had their own unique color scheme and design for their special event. They went shopping with me to pick out the colors of their choice. I crocheted enough kippah so all the male guests had one to wear at the ceremony, and they could keep it as a souvenir of the event. In each kippah, a label was sewn on which was printed the event, the child's name, and the date. I have a drawer full of these keepsakes. I feel elated when I see one of my crocheted kippah worn by someone at my synagogue.

While writing this memoir, I was crocheting for Melanie, my youngest granddaughter's Bat Mitzvah, which was September 24, 2016. It was the weekend before Rosh Ha Shana, the Jewish New Year 5777. Progress! The printed labels are now iron-on. This is much easier, quicker, and more practical than sewing.

Melanie's mother, my daughter, Leah, celebrated her Bat Mitzvah during the holiday of Sukkot. Rema, my sister-in-law, and I made the table centerpieces, a sukkah. A sukkah is a temporary house or hut with a thatched roof. One needs to be able to see the sun in the day and the stars at night through the roof. It is constructed for the week-long festival of Sukkot. Jews eat, study, and sometimes sleep in the Sukkah. This holiday commemorates the time when God provided for the Jews in the wilderness. This is a joyous fall holiday. Many Jewish families build a sukkah in their backyard for this holiday. I have also seen them on apartment patios, especially in Israel.

To make this table centerpiece, we collected Lord & Taylor shirt gift boxes, dowels, Styrofoam coffee cups, fabric, lace, mini baskets, birthday candles, little dark-haired dolls, mini brooms, small artificial fruit, leaves, branches, and gift wrapping paper.

The shirt gift boxes were wrapped in shiny brown wrapping paper to represent the earth. Dowels were glued standing upright at each of the four corners of the gift box. On top of these standing dowels, four more dowels were cut and glued into a rectangle, the same size as the box and placed on top of the standing dowels. Tiny plastic fruits and branches with leaves were threaded and strung across the opened rectangular top. An upside-down Styrofoam coffee cup decorated with a large glittered six-pointed Jewish star became a lectern with an open paper Torah scroll placed on top of it.

Behind the lectern stood a dark-haired doll dressed in the same color dress as Leah was wearing. The doll wore a circular head covering of the same sheer dress fabric. A gold-painted toothpick became the *yad* in the doll's hand. Yad in Hebrew means hand. A yad is used as a pointer, to help the reader keep her place while reading from the Torah. One doesn't touch the sacred parchment of the Torah—made from the skin of a kosher animal—because it can be damaged by the skin oils and perspiration.

On the floor next to the lectern sat a small wicker basket lined with the same fabric as the doll's dress. In the basket was a mini baked clay *challah* (bread for Shabbat) and mini Shabbat candles. A broom rested against one of the upright dowels. Attached to the broom was a thin ribbon on which was printed, Leah's Bat Mitzvah and the date. One of these sukkahs was placed at the center of each of the tables. We received many compliments about our centerpieces. Many of the guests took the centerpieces home.

I belong to my Florida community's knitting/crocheting club. We meet for a couple of hours on Monday and Thursday mornings in the spacious arts-and-crafts room. Everyone is making something different: sweaters, scarves, hats, and blankets from simple to very complex patterns. Many of the women make items for cancer patients or children in hospitals. Others make things for themselves or their precious grandchildren. We are a mix of beginners to experts. There are the regulars who show up all the time. There are the women who come for assistance starting a new project or to get help ending a project. What knits us together are the instructions, the conversation, the caring, the sharing, and the laughter.

Chocolates

These sold well at craft shows and school holiday bazaars. My children and their friends enjoyed me making molded and hand-painted chocolates. The kids got to scrape out the bowls and lick the spatulas before they were washed. When they were finished, their smiles were wide, the bowls were spotless, but their hands and faces need to be cleaned.

Some of these delicious items were decorated chocolate greeting cards for Valentine's Day, Halloween, Christmas, Chanukah, Rosh Ha Shana, birthdays, and Easter. Holiday items: Santas, trees, stars, dreidels, bunnies, and eggs always sold quickly. Lollipops came in all shapes and sizes. I even made x-rated adult lollipops. These were not sold at school bazaars.

An eye-catcher on my display table was a chocolate holiday house similar in design to a gingerbread house. At this two-day Christmas school bazaar, my display table was in a corner directly in front of a large window. It could have been the baseboard heat or the sun shining through the window that melted and collapsed the back corner of the chocolate house into a pooled clump of chocolate. From the front it still looked like a delicious holiday house. So it remained on the table even though it wasn't saleable.

The PTA mother in charge of the event called to tell me about this meltdown before I arrived for the second day of the sale. She felt bad, was very apologetic, and asked what she could do to help. I told her to come to my table at the end of the event. That's when I gave her the house and told her to share it with her committee. It wasn't saleable, but it still was edible and tasted delicious. The committee women came over to thank me and purchased whatever candies that were left on the table. It proves that if you give a little, you usually get something in return.

Some of my craft items went to consignment shops. Others I gave away as gifts. A few were kept and used to decorate my home. Money shirts were the single item that made the most income.

Money Shirt

If this paragraph sounds like an advertisement, it's meant to. I found this kind of soft sell did very well. What is a money shirt, you ask? It is a gift item for the person who has everything. Or it's for someone whose likes and interests you do not know. You tell me how much you want to spend on the gift. I then figure out how many ones, fives, tens, twenty-dollar bills and coins will be needed to equal the amount of your gift. Next, I send my husband to the bank to get an assortment of freshly printed bills or clean unwrinkled bills in different denominations. Occasionally, I have had to iron some money.

A novel Money Shirt gift for the person who has everything.

Once Herm showed his favorite bank teller a picture of the money shirt, she was eager to find the newly printed bills. Using a shirt cardboard from my husband's closet, I arranged the money on it to form a shirt. For a male gift I added a tie and a hankie in the breast pocket. For a female, I attach a lace collar and cuffs. I did charge a fee for making the shirt. My money shirts have been gifted to people as far away as California, Canada, and Israel.

We were invited to our Israeli friend's son's Bar Mitzvah, many years ago. We visit this family every time we went to Israel and they visit us in the States frequently. As part of our gift, we had the son stay with us for two weeks during his summer vacation. He and Adam, our son, were close in age and both enjoyed sports.

During his visit with us, Herm, Adam, and Moshe joined a pick-up baseball game at a picnic we attended. Moshe had never played baseball but was athletic. His first time up at bat he had one strike and then a foul ball. Not knowing the game, he ran to first base on the foul ball. He was told to come back to the batter's box. As he stopped and turned to figure out which way to go he tripped. He extended his right arm out to break his fall. Not only did he break his fall, he cracked his radius, the thinner forearm bone.

Moshe was in a lot of pain. I packed his arm in ice from the soda chest. We called our neighbor, an orthopedist who met us at the local hospital. The x-ray clearly showed the break, even to unprofessional eyes. Moshe's arm was put in a cast. He was given some pain medicine and sent home with us.

That night the boys were going with Herm to a preseason Eagles football game. No way would Moshe stay home no matter how painful his arm was. The three guys had dinner, snack,s and a fun evening at the football stadium that night.

Moshe went home to Israel the following week. His cast had the skyline of New York City painted on it by Herm's younger sister, Rema. We instructed Moshe to carry a jacket over his cast when he disembarked from the plane. After he kissed his mother hello and she saw that he was okay then he could show her his cast and tell her all about his baseball experience.

When we next visited Moshe's family in Israel, the money shirt Bar Mitzvah gift was framed and hanging on the wall in his teenage bedroom. On his bookcase sat his split, painted forearm cast. He had saved and displayed both these souvenirs of his visit with us. Now that he is married and has children of his own, the framed money shirt hangs in the den of his home.

I enjoy knowing that something I made for someone special is still on display in Israel.

Synchronicity! Just this week I received a phone call from a relative of a close friend of mine. Her son had received my money shirt as a Bar Mitzvah gift. The mother said that was the most unique gift her son had received. Those words felt like music to my ears.

Her son had the money shirt in a dresser drawer. I told her if the kid hasn't spent it, why not put it in a frame and hang it on the wall like my Israeli friend did? She liked that idea. The mother called me because she was going to a Bar Mitzvah. She wanted to know if I still was making the money shirt. She ordered three shirts of different denominations.

Zora's ORiginal Arts

I called my craft company Zora's ORiginal Arts. I had business cards and gold oval adhesive labels printed. The labels contained my name, address, and phone number. I adhered them on the back of everything I created.

I was a one-person company. Making crafts filled my empty evening hours with a relaxing, enjoyable, and profitable activity. I found a form of art where color wasn't going to hinder me. I felt proud of being recognized for my creativity.

A Costume

Purim is a Jewish holiday where we dress in costumes similar to Halloween. One year when my son Adam was in nursery school, he wore a costume that I had made for him. It was a purple cloth cape edged with fluffy, fuzzy small purple tassels. On the cape I painted large gold Hebrew letters which said *melach katon* (little king). That cape is now in a memory box with a collection of assorted family souvenirs that are all dear to my heart. I will give this cape to Levi, Adam's son, when he is in nursery school.

Purim takes place on the fifteenth of the Hebrew month of Adar which corresponds to either March or April on our Gregorian calendar. It is a happy and fun holiday that commemorates the salvation of the Jewish people in ancient Persia from an anti-Semitic prime minister named Haman who plotted to destroy the Jewish people by killing them all. This story is recorded in the Book of Esther (Meggillah of Esther) written on a parchment scroll.

This scroll is read in the synagogue on Purim. When wicked Haman's name is mentioned, we shake or twirl groggers (noise makers) to drown out the sound of his name. Adults and children alike don costumes to represent the characters in the Purim story and then parade around the sanctuary. It is a noisy, festive, fun holiday.

Other activities associated with Purim include donating to charity for the poor and sending our friends *mishaloch manot*, gifts of food. The special treat of the holiday which is the main item in the basket of food is hamantashen. This pastry is a flakey, tasty triangular cookie usually filled with prune or other fruit. The triangular shape of the cookie represents Haman's hat.

I included the Purim story here for several reasons. First, we were celebrating the holiday as I started writing this chapter. Second, I feel that I have a historical connection to Jewish royalty. I was brought up as a Jewish princess in Brooklyn. Also, Esther was my favorite grandmother's Hebrew name. And finally, it is a fun holiday where we are allowed to make a lot of noise, be playful, and act silly. Most other Jewish holidays have rules that start with the word DON'T.

Here is a little ditty that flowed from my pen as soon as I finished writing this chapter.

Crafty me, can it be?
A klutz who cannot see.
I even was born a lefty.

A lefty puts me in my right mind.
It gives me the trait of being kind.
No, I am not totally blind!

I find the things that I can do well.
I even make crafts that do sell.
I am happy when my friends do k'vell*

I'm finding myself and beginning to appear.
Inner child, there is no more need to fear.
Together our new convergence we shall share.

Old stories and fears will no longer hold us back.
Together we shall make a new contract.
Then like a magnet positive things we'll attract.

I am beginning to see the skills I possess.
I'm making a change, and this is progress.
It hasn't been easy, I must confess.

I came from behind, now I am leading.
I changed my mindset, now I am succeeding.
Soon everyone my book will be reading.

* *k'vell* a Yiddish word meaning bursting with pride

Creating things promotes psychological well-being. It promotes happiness because when we make, create, or repair things we feel vital, effective, and our self-esteem goes up.

Creativity, Happiness and Hands

It has been shown that hand activity from knitting to woodworking to growing vegetables and chopping them can reduce stress, relieve anxiety, and modify depression.

It is the time you spent on your roses that makes the roses important to you. When you knit, cook, engage in carpentry, or build something, it is the time you devote, the effort and the love you do it with, that makes it worthwhile. It isn't so much what you can do, but what you do! The process itself provides the value.

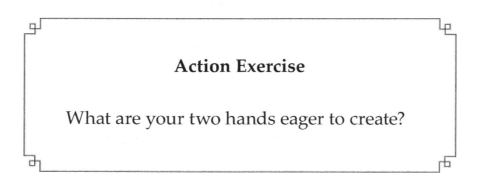

Action Exercise

What are your two hands eager to create?

CHAPTER 6

Zora – A Name

I am aligned with a higher power.

I believe in signs, symbols, and gut feelings. Thus, I am investigating the meanings of my names to see if they influence my personality and thought process. A name is a word used to identify a person, place, or thing. There are popular, ethnic, religious, unusual, and common names.

Zora is my given birth name. I was told that my mother made it up by removing some letters from my Hebrew name, Zipporah. If my given name was Zipporah, I would have been called Tzippy in my Brooklyn neighborhood. My Mom disliked nicknames. I was named for my mother's beloved paternal grandmother. In the book of Exodus, Zipporah is the wife of Moses. In Hebrew *tzipor* means bird. The name Zora has a variety of spellings: Zorah, Zorya, or Zohra. The derivation of the name Zora could be Arabic, Croatian, Bulgarian, Slavic, or Macedonian. It means Dawn or Aurora. It is usually a girl's name.

I have long believed I am defined by my name, Zora. It fits me. It is unusual and unique. People tend to remember it and me. My married name makes it even more unusual. And, of course, there is no other Zora who lives in King of Prussia on Gypsy Lane. Doesn't that sound exotic? I am the self-anointed Queen of King of Prussia. I like to wear my white sweatshirt that says in bold, red letters, **Bow to the Queen.** I also wear a black baseball cap with the word **QUEEN** boldly printed on it. Nobody bows, sometimes they chuckle, but it still makes me feel special.

In graduate school at the University of Pennsylvania during the first roll call, my name was a stopper. The professor announced each student's name alphabetically with a Miss or Mr. in front of it. When he came to my name his face reflected confusion and there was a moment of silence. He didn't know what address to put in front of it, Miss or Mr. or how to pronounce the last name. So, I clearly and loudly announced: "Mrs. Zora Natanblut." The class chuckled. The teacher blushed. Consequently, he never forgot my name.

Estelle

Estelle is an old French name derived from Latin meaning star. My middle name Estelle is for my father's youngest sister who died as a young married woman. I know nothing more than that. My father remained friends with his brother-in-law, who eventually married another Estelle. I knew this Estelle as my aunt and loved her.

Cookie

My nickname growing up was Cookie. I was given it by a baby nurse who I have no recollection of. My parents and Louise never used that nickname. To them I was always and only Zora. My cousins and Uncle Jack called me Cookie. The only time I used the name Cookie was when I visited my cousin who lived in our apartment building on the third floor directly above us. When I rang their doorbell, I said, "It's Cookie." When I send this cousin a birthday card, I sometimes sign it Cookie.

My grandma Erna, my mom's mom, said the name Cookie fit me because like a cookie I was delicious and sweet enough to eat. She should know because she baked the most delicious sugar cookies and pies. Also, my grandfather owned Messing Bakeries and my last name was Messing.

My three names. Zora meaning dawn or aurora. Estelle meaning star. Zipporah meaning bird. All my names seem to relate to the sky or atmosphere and its movement. Everything about my names relates to the flow of what is around me. There is a flow from morning to evening. I tend to be a person who goes with the flow. I never realized how my names followed a skyward theme. A bird makes a connection between the earth and sky.

I am not ethereal, but I am spiritual. I do have a chapter about my Flying Solo. I don't consider myself to be a person with her head in the clouds. However, I do believe in angels, fairies, and spirituality. I feel the connection, do you see it?

When I married, my initials became ZEN. I thought that was cool and symbolic because ZEN Buddhism emphasizes the value of intuition. I depend greatly on my intuition or inner knowing. Because of my vision or lack of it, I am a person greatly influenced by signs, symbols, and sounds. I see more clearly by listening to others' descriptions of objects or scenes. Listening and touching greatly enhances my sight. My world becomes colorful, brighter, and clearer by hearing how others describe what they see.

Famous Zoras

Had my mother read any of Zora Neal Hurston's books? Zora Neal Hurston was a black female writer and leader of the Harlem Renaissance in 1925. She has written an autobiography called *Dust Tracks on the Road*, which was published in 1942. It is the story of her rise from childhood poverty in rural Florida to a place of prominence, as an American writer. Another of her books, *Their Eyes Were Watching God*, Oprah Winfrey made into a TV movie in 2005.

I would someday love to have the name recognition that Zora Neal Hurston does as an author.

Zohra Lampert is an American actress, who has had roles in film, television, and stage. She may be best remembered for her role as the title character in the 1971 cult horror film *Let's Scare Jessica to Death*, as well as for starring alongside Natalie Wood and Warren Beatty in the 1961 romance film *Splendor in the Grass*. This was one of my favorite movies. I have watched it numerous times. I love romantic movies and books.

Zohra Lampert, only three years older than me, was born in New York City, and she graduated from a New York City High School. I was born in a New York City Hospital. I grew up in Brooklyn, New York and graduated from Erasmus Hall High School. Zohra was the daughter of Russian Jewish immigrants. I am the granddaughter of German Jewish immigrants. So we have a few things in common besides our name. I have no desire to be a movie star or an actress. But I would like recognition as an author.

Becoming an author has forced me to reveal my secret in order to move forward in my life. This was an emotional and most difficult revelation for me. I know that I am not the only one with secrets. I found that my secret only hurt and harmed myself. Sharing this has not been easy, but hopefully it will help others to open up about themselves. To me, it feels like a heavy weight has been lifted off my shoulders and my heart.

Another Zora

On the bookshelf in my physical therapy office, I have all of Zora Neal Hurston's books prominently displayed so I and my clients can see my name, ZORA, in print. I also have a book with my Hebrew name in the title, *Zipporah, Wife of Moses* by Marek

Halter, on the same bookshelf. Someday my book, *Who is Zora? Sight Unseen* will be displayed on that shelf also. My vision might not be 20/20, but I can see my book displayed on shelves in libraries, bookstores, and people's homes.

I have been asked if I ever met another Zora. At first, I quickly answered no, I'm one of a kind. Then I remembered a small incident that happened early in my physical therapy career. I was working as a staff PT in a large university hospital. A coworker asked me to see a patient in room 360 bed A. I inquired if I was to treat this patient. She said no. I was just to introduce myself to her. That seemed rather odd to me, but I said that I would do it.

This therapist and I frequently discussed similar cases we were seeing. I usually took over her patients when she went on vacation. So, I didn't give it any further thought. When I was on the third floor that day, I checked out the patient's chart and headed to her room with a big smile on my face. There in bed A was an elderly, plump black lady. I was young, trim, and white. What a contrast!

I walked up to her bed, looked straight into her eyes and introduced myself. "Hi, I am not here to treat you. Your physical therapist asked me to introduce myself to you. My name is Zora." She just stared at me for a minute. I think we both were sizing each other up. Then we simultaneously burst out laughing and giggling. As you probably already guessed, her name was also Zora.

Neither one of us had ever met another person named Zora. We both believed that we were one of a kind. We chatted for a few minutes. I would have loved to have spent some more time talking to her, but my work schedule didn't allow it. Unfortunately, our paths never crossed again.

Eatonville, Florida

On one of our drives down to Florida, we stopped in Eatonville, Florida, Zora Neal Hurston's hometown. A small garage was set up as a museum. On display were pictures by some local artist. That meant nothing to me. I went straight to the gift table. There were so many items with my name on it. I purchased pins and T-shirts. I already had all her books. I signed the guest book. The lady behind the desk looked at me and loudly announced, "Oh Miss Zora." She introduced me to all the staff calling me "Miss Zora, Miss Zora." It made me feel very special. I guess that they don't get many visitors with the name Zora.

I wanted to tour the town Zora grew up in, but it was raining heavily that day.

Coincidentally, when I began writing my memoir, the book I was reading by author Anita Diamant was called *Day After Night*. One of the main characters was called Zorah. This story was a fictionalized version of a post-Holocaust experience. Zorah and her friends confront the challenge of re-creating themselves and discovering a way to live again as a survivor. I am working on re-creating my belief system about who I am: a happy, healthy, successful woman, soon to be a published author.

This made me curious. I wondered were there other books with a character named Zora, in it? I Googled characters in a book named Zora; I did find one.

Zora and Me by Victoria Bond and T.R. Simon. It is a historical novel for seventh graders. The story was inspired by the early life of Zora Neale Hurston. Carrie, the main character, reflects back on her childhood in Eatonville, Florida, with her best friend Zora.

I plan to read it.

Names

Onomastics is the study of names. It includes linguistics, history, anthropology, psychology, philosophy, and more. Etymology is literally the meaning of names. Names are personnel and usually have stories behind then. Jews traditionally name children after beloved deceased relatives. Many children are also named after parents, grandparents, other relatives, celebrities and historical, literary, or biblical characters.

Action Exercise

What is the story of your name?

1. Who named you?
2. Why did they name you that?
3. What does your name mean?
4. Are you happy with your name? If not, what name would you like to be called and why?
5. If you have a nickname, what is it? How did you get that nickname? Do people still call you by that nickname?

CHAPTER 7

Black And White

I acknowledge that everything that happens or doesn't happen is part of my journey.

The Greeks say we should go from alpha to omega. Our alphabet goes from A to Z. Or, as an English Nanny might say, "From A to Zed." English is read and written from left to right. Hebrew is read and written in the opposite direction. Chinese, Japanese, and Korean are written vertically from top to bottom. Directions, colors, and alphabets are the concepts we learn early in childhood.

The majority of people are right-handed. As you have probably already inferred, I am not like most people. I am left-handed. My name begins with the last letter of the alphabet and ends with the first letter. I live in a black-and-white world. I am color blind because I was born with an eye condition called cone dystrophy. Is it any wonder that zebra is my favorite animal? Its name begins with Z and ends with RA just like my name, ZoRA.

Color

I usually mark the labels inside my clothes with abbreviations of the color. Lately, the clothing labels are often a dark color and the magic marker doesn't show up. I find this frustrating because it limits my independence. I hang shirts and blouses on the same hanger as the slacks they coordinate with. Once an outfit is put together I tend to remember what goes with what. I also purchase coordinated outfits of two or three pieces whenever possible.

In another area of life, I believe I dream in Technicolor. I can describe each of the colors in my dream. Is it because intellectually I know that the sky is blue, grass is green, and our flag is red, white, and blue? Who can tell me I am wrong? It is *my* dream!

Or is it because the experience of color is an emotional one just like a dream? Colors can depict a mood or an emotional sensation. Black can represent funereal feelings. Brown reflects earthiness and nurturing. Yellow depicts sunshine and happiness. And red denotes anger, sensuality, or strength. Do you also feel colors as you see them?

This brings up the question of whether black and white are considered colors. It seems this question is one of the most debated issues about color. Ask a scientist and you'll probably get a reply based on physics. Black is not a color but the absence of all color. White reflects light and is the presence of all colors. By contrast, Crayola, the crayon company, considers both black and white to be colors, as do most artists and children.

As a child my favorite joke was: What's black and white and red (read) all over? The answer "newspaper" always had me giggling. And it made my father chuckle too.

Black and white are opposites, just like night and day. My name is an alphabet opposite. I say that I go from Z to A. ZebRA and ZORillA, do also. My friends, ZonnA, ZoannA, ZeldA and ZinniA, have names that share the same alphabet opposite. Maybe we should form our own Z to A club. Like me, most of these women are colleagues who perform some type of hands-on health and healing technique. As a group we are unique by our names and the hands-on work we perform. We are in the field of helping others feel better and improve their health.

As a lefty, it is easier and smoother for me to write Hebrew, which goes from right to left, than English because of the flow. When learning a new skill or exercise I mirror the instructor. Thank goodness, nobody in elementary school tried to switch my left-handedness. Since I am left-handed, I am in my right mind. It is generally right-brained people who are creative. I am revealing this so that you, the reader, can follow my convoluted thought processes with its many detours and digressions.

In high school, I thought it would be fun learning to write with my right hand, thinking it would make me feel and look more like the majority of students. This was one of the ways to blend in rather than stand out. The difference in my visual acuity provided more than enough opportunity to separate me from my peers.

I always sat in the front row—even though I still couldn't read the blackboard. This day, I held a pen in each hand. If I didn't have to concentrate on what was being said, I wrote in script with my right hand. The notebook was held in the portrait position, upright in front of me. It was in the landscape position, ninety degrees sideways, when writing with my dominant left hand. With neither hand did I stay within the lines. When teachers saw me switch writing hands, they did a double-take. I enjoyed their reaction. It took only a semester to feel comfortable and confident writing script with my non-dominant right hand.

Don't you agree teaching oneself to be ambidextrous is creative? I thought that I made very good use of my time in those boring high school classes.

Sports

When it came to sports, all the equipment was for righties. I used my mother's right-handed golf clubs. As a teen, I had no choice but to use a right-handed bowling ball. I still bowl right-handed many, many years later as a senior citizen. When it came to softball, I was a switch hitter. I can't remember how I cradled the ball in lacrosse or if it made a difference. Gym class and the world of sports in general discriminated against lefties at that time.

Gym was a required class in elementary and high school. To avoid participating in sports in high school, I took dance for one semester. That didn't make me feel any better about myself; I was a klutz. Most of the girls in high school who took dance were veritable dancers. Clearly, I was not in my own element in that endeavor either. I was no Maria Tallchief.

At school and camp, softball was the favorite outdoor sport. I hated that game. It made me feel uncoordinated, like a loser, unwanted, and disliked. I was always the last one to be chosen on a team. I often heard teammates saying, not too softly, "Do we have to have HER on our team?" That simple short sentence cut like a knife through my insides.

Usually I was placed in the outfield. I believe that my teammates and I had the same thoughts during the ball game. We simultaneously prayed that the other team couldn't hit to where I was standing. From my position in the bright sunshine of the outfield, I was too far away to see or follow the baseball. I might just as well have been reading a book.

Tennis was a requirement at camp. All I remember about tennis was the counselor yelling "swing" as she tossed the ball over the net towards my racquet. So I would swing with all my might. My racquet caught the air in an upward motion as the ball bounced either to the side or behind me.

I saw the counselor's arm swing as she released the ball. But never saw the ball. This made me want to smash the racquet or the counselor. Being out in the hot, bright sunlight for any reason was and still is most unpleasant. It makes my eyes squint and tear. Ballgames or team sports always made my stomach churn. I learned how to internally brace myself so I wouldn't cry no matter how humiliated I felt. I never mentioned to the coach or my teammates that I could not see the ball, especially if it was moving.

Added to my distaste for, and fear of, playing sports, I was once knocked unconscious by a boy swinging a baseball bat. Objects coming at me, whether I see them or feel them, still scare me and make me cover my head and duck. When friends' hands move too close to my face as they are talking to me, I either step back or I gently grab their wrists and place their hands by their sides.

Another semester I took swimming as my gym class. I was a good swimmer and have always enjoyed it. Two things about swimming in high school that spoiled it for me were the bathing suits and the showers. The school supplied the bathing suits. They were wool tank suits designed as one size fits all. The thought of wearing a bathing suit that other people wore seemed gross. The suits itched and just hung on us. I was so uncomfortable and self-conscious wearing that bathing suit that it took all the joy out of swimming.

Showers after swimming were even more embarrassing than the bathing suits. The shower stalls were in rows with no curtains. The gym teacher sat above the stalls watching to see that we used soap and washed our bodies. This struck me as humiliating, embarrassing, and demeaning. Nobody had watched me shower or bathe since I was a little child. I took only one semester of swimming, even though I loved to swim. I frequently was absent or said I had my period on swim days to avoid the swimsuits and showers.

For me, swimming laps can be meditative. My arms and legs move rhythmically and alternately as my head gently rolls from side to side. As my face comes out of the water, I inhale. I slowly and methodically repeat this pattern as I travel from one end of the pool to the other, back and forth, back and forth. My mind is free and clear. The texture and temperature of the water gliding gently against my body are soothing and calming. I feel comfortably encased in my element of water.

According to Western culture, four elements are considered essential to life. They are earth, air, fire, and water. Water is my element. I like to go with the flow. I enjoy dressing in long flowing skirts and blouses. I am often moved to tears when I read a romantic novel or see a heart-wrenching movie. At times, I can be as inconsistent as the tides, flowing in and out. I have been told that I have a bubbly personality. I enjoy gazing into water: a placid lake, a gurgling stream, or waves at the seashore.

I embody most of the positive personality traits of a person whose element is water. I feel my way through life. Being tactile enhances my sight. My hands feel the finer details of textures, shapes, weight, size, and density of objects. I tend to follow my heart before my brain; I am sensitive, intuitive, empathic, and a good listener.

What bothers me is that I also have some of the negative traits of the water element. I can be too sensitive and have my feelings easily hurt. When I can't see to do something, I get easily frustrated, and tears may flow. In the past, I have been a private and secretive person in regards to my vision. I could not say "I am legally blind" or "I am color blind." I am using this book to help me get over that sensitivity. Even as a senior citizen, I believe in continually growing and improving.

Games

One thing that has stayed the same for me is my enjoyment in playing board games. As a young person, they were way more fun for me than gym and sports. As a young adult, the game of mah jongg was particularly appealing to me. Mah jongg originated in China. It is commonly played by four players. It is similar to the card game rummy. Instead of cards, mah jongg is played with a set of 144 tiles based on Chinese characters and symbols. It is a game of skill, strategy, and calculation that involves a degree of chance.

One of the many designs on a mah jongg tile is a dragon. There are both red and green dragons. My very old and worn set had the dragon tile with two different designs, one for red the other green. Thus, I could distinguish the red from the green dragon easily. But when I would play with other women, they would bring newer mah jongg sets. In these newer sets, the dragon designs were identical except for the color. Obviously, there was no way for me to distinguish the red from the green.

My way around this problem was to avoid playing a hand with dragons. If I discarded a dragon, I would just say "dragon" and not name the color. Someone else usually announced the color, assuming I just forgot to mention it. Though I liked the women I played with, I began having too much angst before playing. So, I just told them that I was too busy to attend the weekly game. I gave my mah jongg set to the local thrift store. That was the end of that! I have not played mah jongg since nor have I missed it.

In hindsight, I now realize if I had just leveled with those friends and revealed to them that I couldn't distinguish colors, they probably would have played with my old mah jongg set. However, at that time it was still too heavy a personal issue for me to disclose.

The only games I play now are dominos, bridge, and canasta. Even though each of these games presents a visual challenge for me, so far I have been able to manage to play. From across the table, I have difficulty distinguishing between the shapes of diamonds (red) and spades (black). I work hard at seeing when I play any games.

As a child when I played games and color was involved, my mother made adaptations for me. If it was a card game, Mom would write the name of the color on the card. In the game of Sorry, I took either the lightest or darkest four men, whichever I could more easily distinguish.

In this chapter, I granted you a brief visit into my mind for a glimpse of my thoughts and vision. A view through my eyes has many limitations: color, clarity, distance, and details. Since these can't be corrected,

I have turned them into an optical obstacle to be circumvented. I don't let these limitations stop me from living my life to the fullest.

My world is one of light, medium, and dark shades. To me white and black are the beginning and end of the color spectrum. I think of them as night and day—the ends of a twenty-four-hour period.

I do better in the night. I like the dark. I find the dark comforting. I am photophobic, so bright lights hurt my eyes. I need to wear very dark sunglasses when I am outside and sometimes, if there is bright fluorescent lighting, inside.

"Yes" is my answer to this chapter's question. I concur with Crayola as well as artists and children—black and white are indeed colors.

Black and White Thinking

Are you a black-and-white thinker? Do your moods constantly fluctuate from great to depressed?

Many people suffer from a black-and-white thinking pattern. It is an all or nothing form of thinking which you probably picked up in your childhood. This kind of thinking affects your sense of self, well-being, happiness, and relationships.

Letting go of this black-and-white thinking is important for your self-growth and happiness. It is a gradual process of letting go of *musts* and *shoulds* in little increments.

Be patient! You begin to accept *what-ifs* and *maybes*. If you fail an exam, it doesn't mean that you are stupid or a failure. Just because you don't come in first in a race doesn't mean all your practice was in vain.

As you realize that extreme black-and-white thinking damages all areas of your life, you are able to make a conscious change. The change must take place gradually. Change happens with small steps.

Action Exercise

Keep a notebook of *woulds* and *shoulds*. Make notes as they become *what-ifs* and *maybes*.

Allow Yourself To:

- Be vulnerable
- Make mistakes and learn from them
- Stop passing judgments
- Stop trying to control outcomes

Allowing ourselves to venture into uncertainty is paradoxically a way to see more clearly, not in black and white or even gray, but in a complex, dazzling rainbow.

CHAPTER 8

My Dr. King

I attract people who help me achieve my goals.

My Dr. King is not the person that probably comes to your mind—a black, male Baptist minister. Rather, my Dr. King is white, Jewish, and female. She is well known and well respected both at Gratz College in Philadelphia and in the field of Jewish education at large. To me, she was a teacher's teacher. She taught and mentored well into her senior years. At the age of ninety, she is happily retired.

Gratz College

At Gratz, I was not the typical graduate student. I was a middle-aged matron, and I definitely wasn't seeking another degree or career. I was already teaching in my synagogue because, while they had students, they were desperate for teachers. They assumed I knew something about Judaism because many years before I started a successful nursery school at this synagogue, and I was its first teacher.

I was willing to start the nursery school because I believed that my son, Adam, and his friends needed a Jewish identity before entering the neighborhood elementary school. The Jewish preschool my daughters had gone to no longer existed. We were living in a very assimilated area. The local preschools now were all church affiliated.

Also at this time, my technical guru husband bought our first home computer, an Apple II. It was an expensive novelty. Computers had entered business and industry but were not yet in schools or many homes. Our children quickly adapted to this technology because we had lots of educational games to entice them. I, on the other hand, was timid when it came to using a computer.

The computer replaced my father's old Remington portable typewriter, which had been relegated to the basement. It had been an old friend, and I thought of it as a backup in case the computer proved to be as menacing as I had anticipated. Fortunately, that was not the case.

The new Apple home computer took up residence on an old Formica kitchen table in the corner of the recreation room next to the back stairs. Herm used the computer for work projects. The kids used it to play games and then eventually for homework. I used it to type reports and papers for work and Gratz College.

It made the work clearer and neater than my left-handed scribble. Through Herm's instructions, I quickly learned the basics: how to turn the computer on and off; how to increase the print size so it was easier for me to read; how and where to file and save my reports so that I could easily find and retrieve them. A new and extremely helpful button to know was called spell-check. That button alone was a major advantage over the typewriter. I didn't have to lug out the huge, heavy *Webster's Dictionary* which always sat near the typewriter. Today, spelling and fact finding are a breeze with Google, Alexa, and Siri close by. No need to fill my bookshelves with A to Z volumes of an encyclopedia any longer.

Of all the computer keys I was learning, SAVE, turned out to be the most important one. I learned about this key through the school of hard knocks. On three different occasions, I lost reports because I closed the computer down before pressing the Save key. After those mistakes the Save key and I became intimate friends.

There was also no longer any use for messy Wite-Out once I found spell-check. Nor was it necessary to print a backup or hard copy of everything I wrote. This was a great improvement over my trusty Remington.

Being the first in our neighborhood with a home computer also made it easy to find a babysitter for Saturday nights!

Throughout my academic life when papers or tests were handed back to me, I scarcely looked at the grade. As soon as I left the classroom, I ripped the paper up and tossed it into the nearest trash can.

Graduating from Gratz College with honors had been truly astounding. Just as I had done before, while at Gratz I rarely looked at the grade on the papers and exams I got back from my professors. Previously, C's were standard, B's were occasional, and A's were an extremely rare grade for me. School had taught me that if I attended class and handed something in when assignments were due, teachers would pass me. All I wanted was to pass and get out of school with a diploma. My parents emphasized learning, recall, and most importantly, knowing where to find information. My grades were inconsequential to them.

I had no intention of getting a degree from Gratz. I was only taking a few courses here and there that interested me. Slowly the credits accumulated without my realizing what was happening. It was my advisor who told me I was about to earn a degree. That, too, was a surprise.

Gratz was a commuter's school. I had neither the time nor the need to participate in any extra activities beyond the classes. However, I did make one close friend. She was a woman about my age getting a degree so that she could teach. We found ourselves in many of the same classes. We often ate a quick home-packed lunch together before rushing off to take the subway into town. We celebrated our Gratz graduation together. We stayed in touch by telephone for a year or so after graduation. But as often happens without a common thread to bind us together, we lost touch with each other.

As an adult, I understood that it is only the diploma employers are interested in. They rarely ask about your grades. Unless you are an honor student, I assume you don't mention grades. I certainly didn't.

I already had a high school diploma from Erasmus Hall, a BA in psychology from Adelphi College, and a graduate degree in physical therapy from the

University of Pennsylvania. I was licensed to practice PT in New York, Pennsylvania, and California though I only worked in Pennsylvania. However, for any young woman in those days, the most important degree was an MRS. That still is my favorite, most prized milestone.

Nevertheless, to this day when I see "with honors" on my diploma, I find myself smiling at the irony of my academic accomplishments.

I must be dreaming. How did that happen? That's impossible! They must have mistakenly confused me with another student. Or maybe, I impressed them with the computer-generated pictures I created as covers for my reports and term papers. I firmly believed in elementary school that if your report had a pretty cover, it seemed to help your grade. Honors just blows my mind even today. Does this mean that I truly am NOT stupid?

I have thought about Dr. King through the years and, finally, thirty years after having been in her class, I decided to send her a note to thank her for being an outstanding teacher, one who was inspiring and in tune with her students. I found her name still listed on the Gratz College website as a current professor.

Here is my letter:

September 4, 2015

Dear Dr. King,

I hope you remember me because I remember you very fondly. You were a very skilled, interesting, informative, and caring teacher. You were my role model when I taught Hebrew school and workshops to therapists. I was a physical therapist before I received my master's in Jewish education in June 1988. In fact, I graduated from Gratz College with honors. Wow, the words "with honors" still seem unbelievable to me.

I read an article in the Philadelphia Inquirer awhile back which said teachers don't always know the effect that they have on their students, so write to tell them. When I thought about all the teachers I had from kindergarten on up through graduate school, few positive memories popped up.

I have been legally blind since birth and as a result school was a very unpleasant experience for me. When I was in elementary and high school, there was no such thing as special help or aides. I also struggled through college and graduate school. By then, I had finally learned how to speak up a little for myself. And when I got my physical therapy license, I swore that I would never return to any school for any reason. It was too humiliating. School was the place that made me feel stupid and inadequate. My needs were neither understood nor met.

When I went to Gratz, I was already a mother of three working as a physical therapist. The first Gratz class I took was with two friends. We all wanted to learn to speak Hebrew. My friends didn't continue taking classes, but I did because Judaism interested me. I avoided education classes. I never wanted to be a teacher. My mom was a science teacher in Brooklyn as I was growing up. She professed to love teaching, but her body language said just the opposite. When she finally went into the family business, she seemed to thrive.

My last year at Gratz, my advisor told me if I would take some education courses,

I would have enough credits for an MA in Jewish education. By this point, I was laughing at myself for being back in school (Never say never!). What did I need another degree for? I was an adult working in a profession I loved. But this school experience was totally different. I felt that the teachers were interested in me as an individual. They saw and heard me. Moreover, this degree made my mother, husband, and children very proud of me. So, it was worth it. It helped me change the way I thought about myself (The Lord works in mysterious ways.).

When I was a child, my maternal grandparents lived near us as did my mom's two sisters and their families. We all belonged to the orthodox synagogue up the block because my grandparents were orthodox. My parents were proud first-generation Americans and were pulling away from orthodoxy, although we did celebrate all the holidays and kept a kosher home.

Since I was "just" a girl who also had visual limitations, my parents thought that Hebrew school would be unnecessary and too taxing *for me. Nevertheless, I did push my parents to send me the year before confirmation. And I have always been grateful for that.*

I am now retired. My three children are all grown and married. I have five grandchildren. We still live in our original house that we purchased in King of Prussia forty-nine years ago. My husband and I now spend our winters in Florida in a senior community. As a retirement project, I have started to write a book about my struggles, my accomplishments and my transformation to self-acceptance.

I believe it all started on the day prior to one of your education classes. You were sitting behind your desk while I was standing next to the desk with my back to the classroom door. The classroom was empty, and we were just chatting. Something you said to me, though I don't recall the exact words, triggered a total meltdown. I felt the wall around me start to crumble. I am sure this happened because I felt safe and had a very strong heart-to-heart connection with you at that moment. I am usually a very controlled person.

Ever since that day, I have been working on giving up the "poor me story." I now celebrate my many accomplishments. Though my vision hasn't changed, I see myself quite differently. Now, I am filled with gratitude for all the things that I can do and have achieved.

I wish to thank you for being there for me whether you knew it or not.

May you have a very healthy, happy, and blessed New Year!

Warmly,
Zora Natanblut

Upon receiving my letter, which had my King of Prussia address, she asked her son to find my phone number. Amazingly, he found my Florida phone number. It was fall, and I was still up north. So, it took awhile before I got her phone message.

A few days before we headed south to Florida, as per habit, I checked my phone and was happily surprised to hear Dr. King's voice. Her voice was just as I remembered. She suggested that we meet for lunch which sounded great to me.

I returned her call and learned that she was still living in the Philadelphia area in a lovely life-care community. She shared that she was ninety years old – but didn't sound like it at all.

Visit with Dr. King

My husband and I arrived at her residence on Tuesday, November 24, 2015 at 12:15 p.m. for our 12:30 appointment. She showed us around her lovely, spacious, fifth-floor apartment. Then we drove over to the main building which housed the café. She insisted on treating us to lunch where the conversation flowed as though we had been friends forever.

Both my husband and I found her amazing. It was hard to believe that she was ninety. She didn't look it. Her eyes were clear. Her skin was smooth. Her mind was sharp. Her posture was erect. Her figure was trim, and her gait was lively. In addition, we learned that Dr. King swims laps about three times a week and makes the ten-minute walk from her building to the main building for meals and events, weather permitting. She is also an active participant in many of the community's committees and activities.

She told us that her husband of sixty-eight years had died the previous year. She loved the community she was living in and had made many friends there. She found it easy to get to Gratz from her new location. She was still driving!

She said she did remember my name because it was unusual. But wasn't certain that she could identify me. However, she said, every teacher wants to receive a letter like mine. Her husband wrote poetry which she kept in a special box with his love letters. She had placed my letter in that box after reading it to her children. I was touched. Her words brought tears to my eyes.

We were given a tour of the gym, pool, dining room, and the large auditorium. As we were touring, a blind man with a white cane was coming down the hall towards us with a careful slow gait, testing the space in front of him with his cane before taking a step. Dr. King went up to him addressing him by name. She said, "Grab my elbow, and I'll take you to the elevator." Together arm in arm they practically sprinted down the hall. Everybody seemed to know her and greeted her warmly as we walked through the halls.

She invited us to join her in the auditorium after lunch for a talk on the latest movies. The speaker briefly and clearly critiqued about twenty-five films. He discussed the themes and the actors' performances.

He shared which ones he liked and why. He also told us which would probably be up for academy awards. His predictions were correct for best picture, *Spotlight*, and best actor, Leonardo DiCaprio in *The Revenant*.

Herm took copious notes of his recommendations since we do most of our movie watching in Florida. Our retirement community usually gets the movies as soon as they have completed their showing in the theaters. That gave us a long list of what to see and what to skip.

It was a delightful afternoon. And we're looking forward to our next visit.

I'm including this chapter in my memoir because of the profound impact Diane King has had on my life. It has been made all the more profound because it took me nearly thirty years to realize how much she has been responsible for some of my most important growth and development. I wonder if without her I'd be so willing to let go of the "poor me" stories I had carried around for so long.

I can think of several people whose long-standing beliefs, attitudes and self-talk have never served them well, and yet they hold onto these as though the resulting behaviors are actually effective. Would I be the same me I was thirty years ago if Dr. King had not come into my life? Sometimes we grow without consciously understanding the impetus behind it.

That day in her classroom so long ago was the trigger that initiated a major change in me. I distinctly remember feeling a physical release of tightly held muscles. The physical sensation I experienced was like removing a tight girdle. It was as though I could actually see as well as feel the wall I had put up around myself breaking apart and crumbling. As my muscular tension began to ebb, the tears stopped flowing. I literally felt lighter. I slowly began to recognize my own accomplishments. The self-image I had carried around for so, so many years was blurring and beginning to disappear.

In thinking about Diane King, I have also become aware of the impact my attendance at Gratz College had on me. My years at Gratz stretched me mentally and emotionally. I enjoyed my studies and research because I picked the topics. Now, that was unusual! Prior to this, my academic pursuits had been a means to an end. The end to me was that important piece of paper, the diploma.

The old adage that "when the student is ready, the teacher appears" has clearly been at play here.

Thank you, Dr. Diane King, for all you have given me. You demonstrated that it is all a matter of where we are at any given time and what we are open to accepting or receiving.

One definition of learning is a change in behavior. You proved to me that I didn't simply attend classes. I truly learned as I became open to change. You also cemented my belief that the universe or *Ha Shem* (The Name) puts that special person in our life at just the right moment. The Yiddish word *bashert* (fated or meant to be) is another way of describing this moment.

Letter Writing

There are many types of letters: business, congratulations, approval, invitations, sympathy, and get well. The nicest letter to receive is a thank you note.

Action Exercise

A hand-written card or note of thanks is one of the most heartfelt, meaningful ways to express gratitude. Maybe you can't repay your recipient for the kindness he or she did for you. Send a note reminding them of what they did and how it physically and emotionally improved the situation and you. Just writing a few words of gratitude will brighten the day for both of you.

Cruising to Remember Louise

I live in harmony with myself and others.

We are returning from a wonderful nine-day cruise to the Caribbean. It is cold and snowy in Pennsylvania but warm and sunny here in Florida as we dock. When we disembark, I inhale one last breath of salt air and sun. Instead of today's to-do list running through my head, I am lingering in the memory of beautiful waterfalls, luscious meals with friends, morning walks around the deck, and relaxing afternoons sunbathing at the pool.

Eight days prior to this cruise, Herm and I traveled from wintry Pennsylvania to warm sunny Florida by auto-train. We enjoy being snowbirds. You won't find snowbird listed in Audubon's anthology of birds. A snowbird is defined as a person who migrates to warmer weather to avoid the harsh northern winter weather. Spending May to October up north and the winters in Florida, we always reside where we can enjoy spring and summer weather.

Our first task after opening our Lake Worth, Florida, home was to empty our suitcases just to quickly refill them with cruise wear: bathing suits, shorts, T-shirts advertising previous cruises, wide-brimmed sunhats, evening wear, toiletries, and plenty of suntan lotion. Everything we brought with us from King of Prussia remained packed until we returned from the cruise.

We were cruising with 136 of our Florida friends and neighbors. Living in Florida makes sailing an easy-access vacation. The hotel, our ship, travels with us. No need to pack and unpack while visiting different locations and sites. It seems to be the perfect form of vacation for seniors. The ship provides us with ambiance, food, and entertainment throughout the day and night. There is always a large gym, spa, and walking loop to help us balance out all the decadent cocktails and desserts we consume.

Land tours at each port are varied for all ages, abilities, and interests from hiking, snorkeling, scuba diving, sunbathing at luscious sunny, white sandy beaches to swimming with stingrays or dolphins. There are also scenic docent-led tours which are usually preceded by on-board lectures about the typography and history of the site. All tours end with plenty of time for shopping, whether it is for expensive jewelry and electronics or island trinkets and T-shirts. Herm usually purchases T-shirts with maps of the area on them.

We have cruised the Caribbean many times before but never to these ports. The well-trained crew pampered us, making our vacation even more special. Herm and I hadn't been on a cruise for two years. On our last cruise, I caught a respiratory cold that took me almost six months to recuperate from. Yes, I did a lot of hand washing and ingesting vitamin C and echinacea, but it didn't seem to have helped. The crew is forever squirting sanitizing liquid into our hands as we enter the dining room, theater, or return to the ship. The crew can also be seen frequently sanitizing stair railings and door handles. However, I have never seen them wiping elevator buttons.

Louise

We chose this specific cruise because of the good friends we'd be traveling with and its destinations: Antigua, Barbados, St. Lucia, and St. Kitts. Day five, Barbados, was the destination calling me the loudest. For that day, we booked a tour to a synagogue that was built in the 1600s. But more than that, Barbados was Louise's home. She was born and buried there. My heart needed to feel physically close to her. From infancy to adulthood, Louise was an important and loving influence in my life.

Barbados was Louise's home, though she did become a US citizen. Louise, as I have previously mentioned, was my family's cook and housekeeper. She had been working for my family before I was born. She was the person who kept our home running smoothly and efficiently. She cleaned, cooked, did laundry, and answered my father's office phone if he was out of the house. Louise greeted his dental patients if they arrived early and Dad hadn't returned from his lunchtime walk.

During these daily walks up Flatbush Avenue, Dad simultaneously took care of business and exercising. He went to the bank, settled his accounts at the neighborhood grocery and drug store, or got a haircut. On Fridays, he would purchase flowers for Shabbat. I remember them being long-stemmed gladiolas, usually white. Louise would arrange the flowers in a beautiful tall, thick, cut-glass vase and place them on the piano in the living room. As I recall there always seemed to be fresh flowers in the living room.

Louise was central to the efficient rhythm of our household. She knew everything about our family, especially our likes and dislikes. In contrast, I knew very little about her except that she was always there Monday through Friday, morning till evening.

Most importantly, she was an avid Brooklyn Dodger fan. Jackie Robinson was her favorite player. When there was a day game, Louise would always have the radio on in the kitchen listening to the play by play announced by sportscaster, Vin Scully.

If the Dodgers were playing in the World Series, it was televised. Our only TV, in my parents' bedroom, remained on during the game even if no one was in this room. Coincidentally, Louise made multiple trips into the bedroom. Then she would report to Dad and his patients the current score.

Louise's weekly routine was to wash the family clothes on Monday. Our apartment building had coin-operated electric washing machines in the basement. The wet wash was hung to dry in the sun on one area of the roof. Here shirts, sheets, and underwear were secured to the line with thick wooden clothespins. I loved the fresh smell of sun-dried sheets and towels. Today's aromatic laundry detergent and dryer sheets don't hold a candle to that fresh outdoors sunshine smell.

On Tuesday and Wednesday afternoons when I returned home from school, Louise, dressed in her pastel cotton maid's uniform, would be standing behind an ironing board squeezed between the stove and the kitchen table. The full laundry basket was on a chair at the apex of the ironing board. The iron sat on a metal plate at the opposite end of the ironing board and was plugged into the wall socket. On these days, Louise ironed everything she had washed: the sheets, tablecloths, and handkerchiefs. My father's shirts and office white coats were crisply starched. Louise even ironed my flannel pajamas and cotton underwear. Every article of clothing was pressed and neatly folded. Then they were returned to their proper closet or drawer for the next wearing.

As I sat at the kitchen table facing Louise while having milk and cookies after school, we chatted. I might tell her about my school day, and she would fill me in on the maids' gossip in the building. We also talked about the Dodgers especially if Robert was with us. Our conversations bounced like a ping pong ball from topic to topic: Dick Tracy and Mrs. Worth, our comic strip favorites; movie stars; an interesting news item; or the weather. These conversations always ended with me asking, "What's for dinner?" Then she would send me off to do my homework.

I don't remember Louise ever being sick or having a vacation. Though I am sure she must have. I knew she loved me and my brother as though we were her own children. She had two young nephews but no children of her own. Louise told us that we were special and frequently praised us.

Robert and I would often ask her which one of us she loved the most. She always diplomatically answered. "Chill'ens, I loves you both the same." Her voice always had a musical island lilt to it. When I was home sick with a cold, Louise always prepared my favorite desserts—tapioca or butterscotch pudding—while Dad would buy me a comic book during his lunchtime walk. Being sick never seemed all that unpleasant to me!

As a little child, my favorite spot to play and hide was against the wall under the baby grand piano in our living room. I was small enough that I could walk under the piano without bending. There I would leave my dolls, stuffed animals and blanket. Louise, whose name I pronounced as "Ou" at that time, helped me hang a small embroidered tablecloth on the piano which was held in place by a heavy, unabridged *Webster's Dictionary*. This became my hideout's door. I was sure that no one could see or find me in my private cozy hideaway.

My dad, as he came into the living room from his office, would ask in a booming voice "Where is Zora?" This always made me giggle. I'd peek my head out and say, "I'm here, Daddy! Here."

Louise would arrive at our apartment about ten a.m. and didn't leave until after the dinner dishes were washed and put away. Sometimes I helped her dry the dinner dishes and put them in their cabinets.

Louise lived on Putnam Avenue and took the Tompkins Avenue bus, which let her off at the Empire Boulevard bus depot, a few short blocks from our home. She always brought the *Daily News* with her in the morning. This newspaper was read by everybody at our house. Robert and I read the comics. My favorites were Dick Tracy, Mrs. Worth, and Little Lu Lu. Louise would change into her cotton uniform before she started her day.

I remember only one time that Louise took Robert and me to the park. The house was her responsibility, not us children. I was little and in a stroller which

Louise pushed. Robert ambled along beside us. We walked the short distance of one apartment building to the corner of Ocean Avenue and Lincoln Road. When the traffic light turned green, we crossed the wide street. Once on the other side of Ocean Avenue, we were in Prospect Park. Prospect Park is best known for housing the Brooklyn Zoo and the Brooklyn Botanical Gardens. I loved both of those places and visited them often.

We walked along the outside of the playground on our right, then around the next corner and under the large stone bridge where Robert and I always yelled, "Hello!" so that we could hear the echo it made. Since it was a warm sunny day, we were headed toward the lake to see the ducks. We brought stale bread with us to feed the ducks and pigeons.

Other times when we were older, Robert and I went to the park to catch tadpoles in the lake. We were hoping to eventually have pet frogs. Frogs were the only thing that Louise was deathly afraid of. Her older brothers frightened her with frogs as she was growing up in Barbados. Just having tadpoles in the house made Louise uneasy. My father saw to it that the tadpoles never became frogs. They quickly and mysteriously disappeared when we weren't looking.

As I reflect back as an adult, I am sure Dad unceremoniously flushed then down the toilet. The only other time we dealt with frogs in our home was when we read about them as one of the ten plagues in the *Haggadah* (The book that explains the story of Passover) at the Passover Seder.

Both of my parents acknowledged that we couldn't have functioned without Louise. My Mom planned the menus, but Louise did the cooking. The aroma from Louise's cooking made your mouth water and your stomach rumble. She could even make vegetables tasty. My grandma Erna taught Louise how to keep a kosher kitchen and Louise strictly adhered to the rules. She and Grandma sometimes shared recipes. It was Louise who changed the dishes, pots, pans, and rearranged the kitchen cabinets at Passover time. She also prepared the Seder meal for the whole *mispuckah* (family) when Grandma Erna couldn't do it anymore.

Our Seder table extended the full length of the foyer and living room. My cousins and I were at the far end away from Grandpa. Grandpa sat at the head of the table reclining on a fluffy pillow as he conducted the Seder by reading and explaining passages from the *Haggadah*. We children knew and enjoyed singing the songs and searching for the *affikoman*.

Affikoman is a special piece of matzah that is hidden by an adult near the beginning of the meal and searched for at the end of the meal by the children. No dessert is served until the affikoman is found and everyone present gets a taste of it. In our house, the children usually were rewarded for finding the affikoman with a "mint sandwich." A mint sandwich was a wax paper sandwich bag filled with coins: a penny, nickel, dime, quarter, and a silver dollar.

I remember one Seder at my parent's house when Amy was a baby. As the Seder was being conducted Amy was in the kitchen with Louise sitting in a high chair. She was happily eating and watching Louise. Our tradition at the Seder was to go around the table so everyone had a chance to read a paragraph from the *Haggadah*. When Amy heard my voice reading she began crying. I brought her into the living room and sat her on my lap at the Seder table with the rest of the family. She was content looking around at everybody and nibbling on a piece of matzah. My lap and the floor around my chair were a mess of crumbs. But I had a happy baby, and that was all I wanted.

Everyone in our extended family had fond feelings for Louise. On warm summer afternoons, Grandma Erna would sometimes stop by with ice cream for

Robert and me. She always had a chocolate ice cream cone for Louise also.

Louise was with my family for over twenty years and yet the only photograph I have of her is a formal one in my wedding album. Louise was black-skinned with twinkly black eyes and shiny black hair which was bobby-pinned up on her head and under a hairnet. She was of average height, stocky build and strong. She always seemed happy, ageless, and had the most infectious laugh I have ever heard.

The last time I saw Louise was prior to her returning to Barbados to be with her family. Chronologically she was an old lady with diabetes and high blood pressure. She was losing her eyesight.

Mom invited her to come on a Sunday afternoon to say goodbye to me, Herman, and baby Amy. We came to Brooklyn for the weekend. It was the only time Louise sat with us in the living room. I don't remember the conversation, only that all of us were feeling sad. Dad called a cab to take Louise home. I walked her out of our apartment and helped her into the taxi. We were both hanging onto each other and weeping uncontrollably. We both knew this was a final goodbye. Not our typical goodnight hug and "See you tomorrow!" We knew we would never see or hug each other again. I promised to write, and I did. When Louise was totally blind, she dictated her letters and a family member wrote them. After Louise died, I continued a correspondence with the family for a while. Unfortunately, over time those letters got lost.

Before our cruise to Barbados, I tried Googling to see if I could find any information on Louise. Regrettably, I only knew her married last name, not her maiden name. I didn't know her age or the date of her birth or death. I do remember her birthday was sometime in the beginning of May, either the eighth or ninth. I didn't know when she came to the USA or where she and her family lived when she returned to Barbados. I realized now how little I knew about Louise. Robert didn't know any of this information either. There was no one to give me these facts. Louise has been gone for over forty years now.

One other small detail I remember about Louise is that on Saturdays she did shampoos at her sister-in-law's Brooklyn beauty parlor. Occasionally, she would wash my long hair in the bathroom sink. I would pretend to be her favorite customer. Her strong fingers would give my skull a delightful massage. She always ended by rinsing my hair in cool water. She told me this closes the pores. To this day, I think of Louise as I rinse my hair in cool water. She towel-dried my long, brown hair and then made two long braids ending in corkscrew curls below the rubber band.

Barbados

Day five of our cruise was to Bridgetown, Barbados. We had planned a land tour of the Kahal Kadosh Nidhe Israel Synagogue (Synagogue of the Scattered Israel) which was built in the 1650s by about 300 Jewish refugees on route to Holland to escape persecution from the Portuguese. Oliver Cromwell opened the English settlement on Barbados in 1627. The Jews arrived and settled there that year. They worked and prospered in the sugar industry. The synagogue was opened in 1654. This was three years prior to England allowing Jews to worship in public.

When the synagogue was destroyed by storms and was rebuilt, a newspaper article in the *Barbados Globe* of April 1, 1833, raved about the building's innovative structure and aesthetically blended classical and modern appearance.

The sugar industry dwindled over the next century. The Jews either left Barbados or converted to Anglicanism. Only one observant Jew remained by the mid-1920s. A team from the Sephardic Temple in London supervised the deconsecrating and sale of the temple. Over the next sixty years, the building's architecture was significantly modified to meet the various new owners' needs. The building was used as a warehouse, headquarters of a horse racing club, a law library, and offices of a wholesale trading company. During this same time, the cemetery surrounding the synagogue which had graves dating back to 1660 was used as a garbage dump.

In 1983, the Barbados government seized the property, wishing to erect a new courthouse on that site. The small Jewish community of about sixty and other supporters of historical structures petitioned the cabinet to turn the building over to the National Trust. It did so in 1985. Two years later, renovation began, and the synagogue was restored to its 1833 appearance. The cemetery with 400 graves has been cleaned, and the gravestones have been repaired. The inscriptions on them are in Hebrew, English, and Ladino (a combination of Hebrew and Spanish).

We had an informative tour guide who took us around the one-room museum. I found it interesting that the floor's surface was a type of Plexiglas that allowed us to see below it. Many small items were displayed under our feet lying in the sand.

The original synagogue had a sand floor. The guide also lectured to our group as we sat on wooden benches arranged around the perimeter of the small Sephardic sanctuary. The congregant benches all faced a central raised lectern, not the Ark holding the Torahs. It reminded me of the layout of the oldest synagogue in America located in Rhode Island.

In 2008, while excavating the former rabbi's house that was on the premises, a mikvah (ritual bath) dating back to the seventeenth century was discovered. The mikvah has been renovated and partially exposed for viewing, but it isn't actually functional. You can peer down into a deep rectangular, tiled bath with its staircase.

Remembrances

I left two remembrances on this synagogue's property. One was a donation in memory of Louise. Barbados was her home, and she is buried somewhere on the island. Secondly, I left a long-handled, wooden kitchen spoon that I ceremoniously placed so that it was hidden under a large leafy bush in a ceramic planter at the edge of the cemetery. To me this gesture symbolized my child-self hiding and playing under the piano. My adult-self saw it as leaving something more personal than a pebble. Pebbles or small stones are traditionally placed on gravesites when visiting a deceased relative or friend.

Why a wooden spoon? This spoon always sat on our kitchen stove in Brooklyn. To me it was Louise's symbol. I am not sure how much she used it to stir things, but Robert and I were very familiar with it. Whenever Louise caught us doing something we shouldn't, she would pick up this spoon in her right hand and shake it at us. She would say one word, "Chill'ens!" That would stop us in our tracks. Robert and I were sure that Louise had eyes behind her head and ears that could pick up our whispers.

Louise now lives only in my heart. I think of her and can feel her presence when I polish my mother's dairy silverware which I use every day in Florida. After I was married, I would call Louise for recipes even though I owned both *Jenny Grossinger's Cookbook* and *The Joy of Cooking*. *Jenny Grossinger's Cookbook* was a perk I received for honeymooning at Grossinger's, a famous kosher hotel in the Catskills. Unfortunately, the hotel no longer exists.

Louise made the best chopped liver. When I helped, my job was to grind the cooked chicken livers, hard-boiled eggs, sautéed onions, schmaltz (rendered chicken fat) a shake of ground pepper and kosher salt together in an old-fashioned metal meat grinder that screwed onto the kitchen table's edge. Louise chose and attached the appropriate size grinding wheel. A bowl was placed below the wheel to catch the chopped ingredients. I also have the hand-held eggbeater Louise always used. There were no electric kitchen tools when I was growing up.

You have probably figured out by now that I am clearly a sentimentalist. Although I don't use it anymore, I still have that meat grinder in my kitchen cabinet in King of Prussia. Presently all my kitchen equipment is electric: mixers, blenders, juicers, and choppers. However, if you were to look into the back corners of my kitchen cabinets and drawers, I'm sure you will find a hand-held eggbeater, handled choppers, and glass reamers for squeezing orange juice. I have seen the same model meat grinder and the other antiquated kitchen items for sale at thrift shops and flea markets. And though I don't use them anymore, I am not ready to part with them.

On shelves packed away in our basement, I have my mother's collection of antique and unusual rolling pins. This collection used to hang in the kitchen of our Brooklyn apartment. I remember watching Louise dusting them. Long ago, I thought about hanging them in my kitchen. But thanks to Herm's logical arguments, that never happened.

I first phoned Louise for recipes when I was a senior in college. Herm was coming to pick me up from Adelphi College and take me home to Brooklyn. I decided to make him dinner. So I called Louise and asked how to make chicken soup. She told me what I needed. I bought the ingredients and put the soup up on the small gas burner stove. I also bought a pre-roasted chicken and made a fresh vegetable salad. While the soup was simmering I took a nap.

When I awoke, the soup had boiled away. There were only dried vegetables and chicken bones stuck to the bottom of the pot. I called Louise in a panic. She laughed, then calmly and wisely suggested that I clean the pot and buy a can of chicken soup.

As it turned out, Herm never came for dinner that night. He was living and working in Philadelphia. That night after work he drove home to Brooklyn in his first self-purchased car, a brand-new stick shift, green, four-door Volvo. This was his first experience driving a stick shift. He was driving three hours on the expressway and the turnpike to his parent's house in Brooklyn. He was afraid of getting stuck in a traffic jam and having to shift gears, which was new for him. He did make it home safely with no problems.

However, he was too exhausted to drive another hour each way to pick me up and then bring me home to Brooklyn. So he came the next day. We had matzo ball soup, chicken, and salad for lunch before returning to Brooklyn.

We both survived my first cooking experience and his driving a stick shift. All was well! A month after I graduated from Adelphi College, we became Mr. and Mrs. Natanblut. Louise of course was a guest at our wedding.

Louise, Zora's second mother.

Before leaving Barbados and returning to our ship, we walked through the gift shop area. We bypassed all the Diamond Exchange stores. The T-shirt shops attracted Herman. I had enough beach cover-ups, T-shirts, refrigerator magnets, and coffee mugs. I needed something that would remind me of Louise and Barbados. After much searching, I finally found the perfect remembrance item: a white ceramic spoon rest. The bowl of the spoon rest had a bouquet of island flowers and the scripted word, Barbados. I also purchased a matching dishtowel. Our kitchen was Louise's domain, so these items seemed appropriate to me. My mind's eye can see her wooden spoon in this spoon rest.

Such a small addition to my Florida kitchen probably wouldn't even be noticed by my guests, especially since these items blended in with the white stove. The spoon rest is on top of the stove and the dish towel is draped over the oven handle. But it makes me feel that Louise's essence is still with me. The older I get, the more sentimental I become. How could I not love this woman? Louise loved Robert and me unconditionally. We were her "chill'ens!"

Honoring a Loved One

Action Exercise

- Make a donation to a charity in their honor. In honoring them, you are also helping someone else.
- Plant a tree in their memory.
- Light a candle and say a prayer in their memory.
- Hold on to a keepsake of theirs. (I had Louise's wooden spoon).
- Speak about them frequently. Write their story.
- Live your life in a way that would make them proud of you.
- Know that you were blessed by having had them in your life.

CHAPTER 10

My New Glasses

I always focus on what is most important at the present moment.

Have I found the miracle that I have been waiting for all my life? Or is it just another bubble that I keep inflating until it bursts, like my dream of having 20/20 vision? During my school years from kindergarten to college, there were no special visual aides that helped me.

Visual Aids

When in graduate school learning to be a physical therapist at the University of Pennsylvania, I had a pair of glasses to which I could attach a telescope to the left lens, which is my stronger eye. It helped me to see what was written on the blackboard some of the time. However, it only let me see what was directly in front of me, only two or three letters at a time. The process of deciphering and reading took an immense amount of effort. If I was copying words off the blackboard, I wasn't listening to what the professor was teaching. The device was helpful but not practical to use. Yes, I did feel self-conscious wearing these glasses. Luckily, it was a small class. After a few odd looks and inquiring questions from my classmates, they just accepted my funny telescope glasses.

Today, we see dentists and surgeons wearing double telescope glasses all the time. My glasses had a heavy black metal frame to support the lenses and telescope. The lenses were two inches wide and one-and-a-half inches high. The left lens had a half-inch circular cut out for the telescope to be screwed into. The hole was near the top of the frame and closer to the nose than the midline. The heavy metal telescope was 2 inches long. I could also put the telescope on a chain or string and wear it around my neck. It was more convenient and less conspicuous to use it this way without the glasses. When the telescope was connected to the glasses, the glasses became lopsided. It would cause the nose pads to cut into the left side of my nose. There was a Velcro strap that went from the glasses' temple earpieces around the back of my head to the other temple earpiece to keep the glasses from slipping.

When first learning about telescope glasses, I was optimistic that they would work wonderfully for me. However, after time they ended up in the dresser drawer. I did take just the telescope with me to the theater and on nature walks. It was smaller than fancy opera glasses, which I was accustomed to using. In theory, the telescope glasses were a great idea, but not practical for my use in the classroom. The sight range of the telescope was very small, and it was heavy.

I presently have a lighter, plastic Nikon telescope on a string worn around my neck. I use it at the theater and at the bowling alley to read the overhead electronic scoreboard. If someone at the bowling alley asks me what I am doing, I usually respond, "I am looking at naughty pictures," a line stolen from the show, *Oklahoma*.

Newspaper Article

There was an article in the *Philadelphia Inquirer* about a high-tech headset which employs a tiny camera that sends high-resolution video through a computer and back to small LED screens in front of the viewer's eyes. Rather than magnifying objects, it breaks them down digitally and sends them back so that a severely visually impaired person can interpret them in real time. According to the company, this does not help the totally blind. It works for about three-fourths of people with low vision. Am I part of that group? I surely hope so.

Just thinking about the possibilities my heart is beating faster and my hands are beginning to sweat. The word *anticipation* is going round and round in my head.

After thoroughly reading that newspaper article, I immediately went on Google and researched the company. eSight is a Canadian company. A pair of their glasses is extremely expensive. Wouldn't you know, the glasses are not covered by medical insurance.

I called the company to find out if they had outlets in the US. They don't! But, they do have a representative in Florida who can demonstrate the glasses. I immediately telephoned and made an appointment. The earliest date for the next appointment was two weeks away.

The demonstrator would come to my Florida home. I had two weeks to ponder if this was a pipe dream. Would it work for me? How difficult would they be to operate? Could I insure these glasses? How heavy would they be on my face?

I still have concerns about what people will think when they see me wearing these odd-looking glasses. If the glasses work, who cares what people think! I never thought that I would say that. Boy, writing this memoir has really helped me to change my thinking, just as I had hoped it would.

If they worked, I would wear them, no matter how goofy they looked. I have to keep reading what I just wrote. It doesn't sound like me. Thank goodness! I guess you can teach an old woman new behaviors.

Zora's Driving

Many years ago, when we were young, daring, and childless, Herman drove me to a local office parking lot at dusk when it was vacant. He let me have a turn behind the wheel. We switched seats. He sat in the front passenger seat next to me. There were no seatbelts in those days. He sat calmly and never flinched as I drove at a snail's pace making wide left and right turns. I tended to be quite heavy on the brake, so we would jerk to a stop.

This was a one-time experience. Please don't report me to the police. I remember it being totally thrilling and scary simultaneously. The same sensation I felt when Herm and I as teenagers rode the Cyclone roller coaster in Coney Island. That too was a one-time experience for my queasy stomach and me.

Now, the only cars I drive are bumper cars on the boardwalk or at amusement parks. There I always drive myself. As you know, the object of bumper cars is to crash into other vehicles. I can do that confidently! All my children and grandchildren love this ride, especially, if they can crash into either Grandma or Grandpa.

As soon as my children passed their driving tests, they became my chauffeurs, especially if they wanted permission to use the car. Now my grandchildren chauffeur me. I tell friends that my *ketubah* (marriage license) which is written in Hebrew, says that I married Herman for better, for worse, and for transportation. Nearly six decades later, he is still chauffeuring me around. He is much better than Lyft or Uber, and there is no charge.

Glasses Demonstration

Although it seemed like forever, the two weeks finally passed, and it was time for my eSight demonstration. I tried not to get too excited or build my hopes up too high. I wanted the glasses to be a panacea for me. Yet,

I knew the chances were slim. From childhood, I was told that my sight was my sight; it would probably never get better and hopefully not get any worse. This statement has proved to be true so far.

Nothing I had been offered as a child improved my vision. The telescope glasses weren't practical for me. Why should there be any difference here? Moreover, these glasses are ridiculously expensive, as I have previously mentioned.

My appointment was scheduled for the same date as my father's birthday, December 8. Now that struck me as a positive omen. My dad was always a cockeyed optimist. Thus, situations always seemed to work out smoothly for him. Linda, a Florida optician, arrived at our house and introduced herself and the eSight glasses. She had me do both a reading and a distance eye test without any glasses to get a base level on my vision. Then she gave me the eSight glasses to try on.

When the eSight glasses are turned on, a disclaimer comes up stating: *Not to be used for driving or other dangerous activities.*

The law does not allow a person who is legally blind to drive. My card from the PennDOT looks like a driver's license but is actually a photo ID. The back of this laminated card states **Identification Purposes**

Only - NOT a Driver's License.

They fit like glasses, but they didn't look like normal glasses. The cameras and internal mechanism made them feel heavy on my face. The nose rests weren't padded and cut into the skin of my nose. Adjusting the magnification and the angle of the glasses took a while. Wearing them for more than a few minutes at a time made me feel a little nauseous. This disappeared as I increased my use.

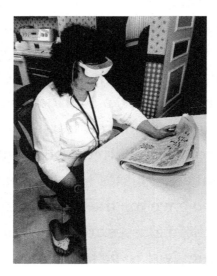

Zora reading the newspaper with her eSight glasses.

When adjusted correctly, reading newsprint was a breeze. eSight helped me identify playing cards that sat across the large kitchen table. Wearing them while walking, meant that I had to look under the glasses to see the ground. The glasses distorted the spatial relationship of my feet and the ground.

I carefully ventured outside my house into the bright Florida sunshine. Linda told me that sunglasses could be worn under these to block out the bright sunlight. I am photophobic. To my delight and amazement, I could clearly read the street sign on our corner. I also could clearly read the house numbers over the garage of the house directly across the street from me. This blew my mind! I was amazed and thrilled! I am unable to read those house numbers even when I am on the sidewalk directly in front of that house.

Watching television, walking, and riding my bike while wearing these glasses will clearly take some mastering. An hour was really not long enough to determine how well these glasses will work for me. The cost is also a great concern. I believe I need more trial time before making a decision to buy them. Both Linda and I felt that I was a good candidate for these glasses. I requested more trial time.

Instead of a demonstrator coming to my home, for my next appointment we drove to an office in Ft. Lauderdale. Traffic wasn't heavy; however, I was feeling apprehensive and nervous as Herm drove the forty-five minutes to meet a different representative. I would be trying an upgraded version of the glasses, which had been reduced by $5,000. Here was another good omen. However, they were still expensive.

As a distraction from my nervousness, I busied myself with crocheting a blanket during the drive there. Our community's knitting group makes lap rugs for nursing home patients and baby blankets for hospital newborns. This was one of those blankets for a donation. I am using up some of the skeins of wool I have lying around the house. Crocheting or knitting keeps my hands and mind occupied as I am a passenger in a car or watching some show on TV. It is a good and productive use of my time.

The tiny, unimpressive eSight office that we met at was a rented room in a large commercial building. We had to wait to be seen because an elderly couple had come in before us. In actuality, their appointment was for the following week. Rob decided to see them because they had a long drive. This put everyone behind schedule. Since I am retired and sometimes forgetful myself, I forgave the elderly couple.

Rob met us in the waiting room. He introduced himself and then led us down a narrow hall to his office. The small office was completely filled by a desk and two visitor chairs. Rob's desk and swivel chair faced the door. We sat in front of the desk facing him. On the upper half of the wall behind Rob were two large windows. The shades were open, and the bright warm Florida sun was shining in on us.

Rob started the interview by asking me to tell him about myself. I gave him just the basic facts that I thought he might need to know. I told him that I was born legally blind. None of my children or grandchildren have any eye problems. I mentioned that because of my vision, school was an utter nightmare for me. I didn't add that this caused me to have very low self-esteem. I also told him that I am a retired physical therapist. We are presently living in a retirement community in Florida, and we love the lifestyle. Rob mentioned that he too lived in the Lake Worth area. If I decided to do a month trial with the eSight glasses and had a problem, he could come over and help me out. That sounded encouraging.

Rob then gave me the standard eye tests. I scored 20/200 just as I always do. He then showed us the new model eSight glasses. This model was white, which I liked better than the black one. These glasses felt lighter. The battery in the remote control was lighter and trimmer. These were both major cosmetic improvements for me. The glasses produced a lot of heat from the vented top. What a strange feeling!

As I previously mentioned, I was sitting facing the window. The shades were pulled back. The sun was very bright. Even though I was still wearing my sunglasses, I politely asked Rob to close the shades because the sunlight was making me squint. "I'm photophobic." I shocked myself by asking for what I needed.

Normally, I would have just sat there and said nothing. Rob's back was to the window. He couldn't see me squinting under my sunglasses. He got up and closed the shades immediately. It wasn't a problem for him.

What a huge step forward for me. I am learning that it is important and totally appropriate to ask for what I need!

There was only a half hour remaining for me to try out the glasses. I read the fine print on a small medicine bottle which I had brought with me. It was amazingly clear and enlarged. I read a newspaper while holding it at a distance most people would. Wearing the eSight glasses, I walked from the office into an elevator and then outside the office building to the parking lot. I attempted reading license plates on cars parked across the lot. I had to find the license plate and then adjust the dials for distance, clarity, and magnitude so that I could distinguish the numbers and letters on the plate. This was as *amazing* to me as reading the house numbers from across the street.

Before we knew it, it was time for Rob's next appointment, and we had to return his sample glasses. This was still too short a trial. We made plans for me to have a month's trial using the glasses. The next pair of glasses the company made was specifically for me because I made a trial commitment. It would take about three weeks. They would mail the glasses directly to my home. That meant more waiting and anticipation.

As the three weeks neared, I called eSight to find out when the glasses would be delivered since we were heading up north to our Pennsylvania home for the Passover Holidays. Not wanting the glasses delivered to an empty house in Florida, I requested that they deliver them to Pennsylvania. The ten-by-fourteen-by-fourteen-inch heavy white cardboard carton with the eSight logo on it arrived late Monday afternoon prior to Passover. I was in the midst of cooking dinner for that night. I took the carton up to my bedroom so that nobody would see it. I didn't want to have to explain things until I was comfortable wearing the glasses.

I had twenty guests coming for the Seder. Seder is a special meal eaten on the first two nights of Passover. We retell the story of how God freed the Israelites from Egypt. We eat symbolic foods such as matzah (unleavened bread), *charoset* (chopped apples, nuts, and wine), and bitter herbs.

When I opened the carton, it was like a never-ending birthday present. There were boxes and zippered cases with more zippered pockets inside. Each space held batteries, cables, straps, glass cases, and an assortment of attachments for the glasses. There were large printed wall charts, a variety of word, number, color, and picture eye charts, and four different manuals. Nothing seemed to be missing!

The manuals included information on the software, safety information, a user's guide, and the thickest one was an eSkills Proficiency Program. I am working my way through that manual now.

eSight Support

The day after the box arrived, my eSight support person in Toronto, Canada called. We set up an appointment for a Skype meeting. It would be an hour session helping me to become familiar with the eSight glasses and how best to use them. Cara would answer any questions that I might have.

During the Skype meeting, Cara spent about ninety minutes with us. Herman was present as my backup. He attached the glasses to Wi-Fi following Cara's directions. I then was given an eye exam with and without the eSight glasses. Cara was able to see what I saw through my glasses using the Wi-Fi connection. She directed me on changing the print size and focus for a clearer view.

During the eye exam, I had trouble reading the last row of numbers because they were a light color on a light background. I had to remember to tell Cara that I was colorblind. She might have realized this because I mentioned seeing something on the news that night about a grandfather receiving glasses that allowed him to see color. I asked her if she could find that information for me. She mentioned that she was interested in getting a pair of those glasses for a colorblind family member of hers.

We covered a lot of ground in our first Skype session. It was intense but well-paced. Cara had a calm, efficient, caring, and friendly demeanor. Her directions were clear, and her listening skills were excellent.

I had another session with Cara a few days later. I reported to her that I was working with the manual to learn how to manipulate all the dials and buttons. There are ten in all. I was using the glasses to read the newspaper in the morning at breakfast. So far, I only used them in my home. I could wear them for about an hour at a time. They are fatiguing for my eyes and heavy to wear. When I remove them, I usually have a red mark across my forehead and an irritation on the bridge of my nose.

Cara told me that I was progressing nicely. She suggested that I speak to Tim, a technical support person who himself wears eSight glasses. Tim called the next morning. I told him that I would be going away for a week on a writer's retreat in Costa Rica and would need to use the glasses with a laptop computer. I was not on familiar or comfortable terms at this point with either piece of equipment, glasses or laptop. During this first phone call, Herm was by my side to interpret the computer lingo. I still was learning how to use the zoom, focus, and contrast knobs. Terms like Wi-Fi and HDMI were still unfamiliar to me.

Herm is far more computer savvy than me and could follow the conversation better. Tim spoke mostly to him during this session. This gave Herm a chance to try the glasses and connect them to the laptop computer.

I made another appointment with Tim two days later. He would call on my cell phone. I would not be able to call him the following week when I was in Costa

Rica. There was so much that I needed to learn about the laptop and the glasses. There was so little time. I was going to a writing retreat where I knew no one. I had to be able to use this unfamiliar laptop with these relatively new bionic glasses.

This would be my first public appearance using them. I had a lot of concerns. I didn't want to have to write in longhand. I am a lefty and do not have a neat handwriting. Sometimes if I write in a hurry, I have trouble deciphering what I wrote. I had to master the computer and the glasses during this phone session. Tim was very patient and encouraging.

There were two more days to play with the glasses and laptop before leaving for Costa Rica. I was very concerned about working with this new equipment without any backup. Herm is usually my right-hand man. He is calm, patient, efficient, and a computer expert. But he wasn't coming to Costa Rica with me. I was "flying solo" for the week.

Back in Florida, I had put the laptop away. I was back to my desktop computer that is more comfortable. The print is large. So there is no need to use glasses of any kind. The controls and keys are all familiar. I felt comfortable writing. I spoke to Tim once a week now. His knowledge and advice were extremely helpful.

I was wearing my eSight glasses out in public if accompanied by a friend or relative. People looked but rarely asked me about them. These glasses are far from a glamour statement. I felt self-conscious wearing these glasses in public. The plus of wearing these glasses meant I had finally given up my life long secret by publicly acknowledging that I had a major vision problem.

These glasses were a great assistance in the supermarket to see prices and read ingredients. I spent a day in the shopping center with a friend, and I wore them the whole time I was there. I could read the size of clothes, where the clothes were made, and the laundry instructions. I could read prices on the cash register and on my receipt.

I have worn them at museums and been able to read the small print on the walls and in showcases. Thus, my husband doesn't have to read to me any longer. I can watch TV sitting back on the couch next to Herm instead of directly in front of the screen blocking his view. I start my day by reading the morning newspaper using them. Being able to do this just brightens my day.

After this month's trial, I was hooked. I now own my own pair of eSight glasses.

My philosophy is, if you are going to dream, dream big. Pipe dreams sometimes do come true.

Dream Big

Dreams are not just for bedtime. A dream is the desire for something new and essential in your life. So dream big, aim high, and plan small. Break down your goals into smaller ones and then tackle each individually. Your abilities enable you to accomplish your goals successfully.

By following your dreams, you can change negative thoughts into a positive mindset. This leads to changing old habits and behaviors.

When working toward goals, it is important to track your progress. If you aren't doing well, it's time to reassess and see what you can do to keep improving. You may not be where you want to be, that's okay. Sometimes things are not as easy as we thought them to be. You just need a little more time.

Don't try and do it alone. Ask friends and family for help or hire a coach.

Every successful person has faced failure. **Learn from your mistakes and know they are just part of the process.** You need to be prepared to work hard, take action, and keep pushing through when things get tough.

Action Exercise

- What is your big dream?
- Write down your goals. Read them frequently.
- Small steps over time will lead you to reaching your goals.
- Record each small step.

Remember to always believe in yourself and Dream Big!

CHAPTER 11

Challenges and Accomplishments

I feel empowered by what I have accomplished.

Dad's Assistant

As a child, I enjoyed helping my father in his darkroom developing dental x-rays. This narrow, utilitarian closet-sized room with a door at either end connected our home to his dental office. One wall contained a kitchen countertop with a large laundry sink near the office end. Above the counter was a storage shelf the length of this tiny room. A narrow, free-standing bookcase was against the opposite wall. There was just enough room for the two of us to stand in the middle of the room. When working, I was perched on a thin stepstool because the counter was higher than a kitchen counter, enabling Dad to work standing up.

When we were developing, both doors were tightly closed, and the incandescent ceiling light was turned off. A bare, red light bulb hanging by its cord dully illuminated the room. To me, it made the room feel like a secret hideout. I see better in the dark than in bright light. It was comforting to have my father standing next to me. We were standing so close without touching that I could feel the rhythm of his breathing and the slightest movement of his body. Dad dubbed me his darkroom assistant. I was enormously proud of that title. I was doing a grownup's job and being acknowledged for doing it well.

There were four liquid solutions, each in a clear rectangular glass container on the counter. Dad removed an exposed x-ray from its light-proof packet. He gingerly held the x-ray by its edge as he attached a stainless-steel x-ray hanger clip to it. He handed the clip to me, and I did the dipping while he did the timing. The first solution was for developing. The second dipping was a rinse water to slow down the developing. When Dad said move on, I put the x-ray in the fixing solution. The final container was for washing all the chemicals away. When that was completed, I hung the clips on the edge of the shelf in the order that I had been given them. Here the x-rays dried before Dad viewed them. We did each patient's x-rays separately. Helping my dad made me feel very grown-up, useful and important. I felt I truly was his best, albeit only, assistant.

After Dad retired, my parents moved to Florida. My brother, my husband, and I helped them clean out their Brooklyn apartment. My folks had moved into this building when it was brand new and lived there for almost forty years. In my father's desk was a file folder with my name on it. More than a little curious, I peeked in. As could be expected, there were my birth certificate and legal name change papers. He had saved a few postcards I sent from summer camp and notes I mailed from college.

I also discovered that my sentimental father had placed the two six-inch-long, thick corkscrew curls that hung below the rubber band that secured my childhood braids in a little gift box. He pasted a small, square, gummed label on top of the box. The hand-written label read: MY LITTLE GIRL IS GROWING UP.

Mr. Scissortail

Most surprising of all was my "Mr. Scissortail Story" which he had cut out from my sixth-grade class newspaper. Mr. Scissortail had been my pet goldfish.

I hadn't thought the story was anything special, just another school assignment. Everyone in my class had a story printed in the end of the year newspaper. It was part of our sixth-grade graduation exercises. But Dad must have thought it was special. Unfortunately, I couldn't ask him about it because at this point he was suffering from Alzheimer's. Nevertheless, I was delighted to learn that he had saved my little story.

The fish tank had been in my bedroom atop a gold-painted rectangular metal fish tank stand. The bottom of the tank was filled with colored gravel surrounding a large piece of white tree-shaped coral, with multiple branches spreading out in all directions. The landscape also included a curved stone bridge. The large fish would swim over the bridge, while the little fish would hide under it. A bush of water greens for the fish to nibble on swayed gently as the fish swam by and would cause the water to ripple. Two snails crept slowly along the glass. They were the sanitation system. There were no lights or aeration system. We changed the water and cleaned the tank every two weeks.

Mr. Scissortail had a long, iridescent body. His graceful tail seemed about as long as his body. He often rooted around in the colorful gravel, and I presumed he enjoyed doing that. He had a wife, Mrs. Scissortail, and two children, Susie and Johnny. Mr. and Mrs. Scissortail never had first names. Isn't that odd? Maybe not really. As a child I was taught to call all adults Mr. or Mrs. followed by their last name. Mrs. Scissortail was plump and whitish with a thin tail.

The fish children didn't last as long as their parents. They would usually end up dead, floating at the top of the tank. After a mini funeral service, they were unceremoniously flushed down the toilet. It seemed that we were yearly replacing Susie or Johnny. This meant a visit to F. W. Woolworth's Five & Dime Store, which was a mere ten-minute walk up Flatbush Avenue.

The pet department, where the goldfish, gravel, and green plants were sold, was all the way in the back left-hand corner of the store. To get there I always meandered through the candy and toy sections. I did this to check out if they had added any new items. Perhaps this was the beginning of my fascination (and possible addiction) to shopping.

When Mr. Scissortail died, I put him in a cardboard jewelry gift box on a fluffy, white cotton square. I thought about mummifying him, like the Egyptians did with their dead, but I was afraid to touch him. So, I covered him with kosher salt. I thought that that would preserve him. Then I wrapped the box in tin foil. I took the box and a shovel across the street to Prospect Park. Mr. Scissortail is buried under the first tree on the right after going out from under the "echoing" bridge. I thanked him for being my pet before burying him. There were no more pets after that. The empty fish tank, with the bridge, gravel, and coral remained in my bedroom for a long time.

A Fishy Tale

Sharing this fish story brings to mind another story from my youth. This incident took place when we were on a family vacation in Cape Cod. I was about eight at the time. Mom took my brother and me out on a fishing boat for half a day. My father stayed onshore, because boats made him seasick. My brother, Robert, three years my senior had a brand-new fishing rod and reel – a birthday present which he was beyond proud of. I used a drop-line with an opened safety pin on the end of it. My bait was stale bread. Robert used worms for bait. Girlish me wouldn't touch the icky dirty wiggly worms.

As you probably anticipated, I was the one who caught the fish, three of them as a matter of fact. I graciously let one of the boatmen remove my fish from the line. Even my mom caught a fish. But Robert caught NOTHING! NADA! I have never let my brother live that down. I'm including this anecdote because, sixty-plus years later, I still believe it's my sisterly duty to antagonize him.

In my mind these two accomplishments—being Dad's assistant and catching those unfortunate fish—represented the sum total of my childhood accomplishments. Graduating from high school, college, and graduate school were like birthdays. They were just passages that are the same for most people. As a child, I did nothing special. I just was a good, quiet, little girl who was to be seen but not heard. And most of the time, when not with family, I tried to make myself invisible. My adult life seemed equally mundane to me. Even the joy of my roles as a daughter, sister, wife, mother, and grandmother did not strike me as anything out of the ordinary.

Special Birthday

When my sixty-fifth birthday was approaching, I decided to change my ordinary life into an extraordinary one. In my mind, it was about time. It was the right time for me to determine "Who is Zora?"

I made certain to create challenges and celebrations in as many aspects of my life as I could. I included physical, spiritual, emotional, financial, and intellectual opportunities to participate in. Even though many of my friends thought I was crazy to do these things, I was excited at the prospect of making this "ZORA'S YEAR."

Physically, I engaged in walking, swimming, and skiing. One of the best side effects of these activities was the loss of forty-two pounds and wearing clothes that were several dress sizes smaller.

Walking was my major physical activity for the year. I signed up for several marathons. The three-day sixty-mile Philadelphia Breast Cancer Walk was the most challenging physical activity of the year. I did that in memory of Rema, my sister-in-law, who had lost her heroic battle with cancer.

Rema

One of my favorite shopping buddies was my sister-in-law, Rema, of blessed memory. Rema has been gone almost seven years, and I miss her dearly. There are times when I still talk to her as though she were beside me. We spent a lot of time together and enjoyed each other's company and friendship. We both felt more like sisters than sisters-in-law.

Rema was an eight-year-old camper during my second summer as a counselor at Camp HES. The letters HES stood for Hebrew Education Society. However, all the campers and counselors knew these three initials meant: Happiness Every Summer.

Rema and I initially bonded when I gave her a large bag of assorted plastic bugs. I always thought she was sweet, even though she also had a cute, devilish side. She secretly placed these plastic bees, wasps, spiders, tarantulas, and assorted other creepy crawly things in her bunkmates' and counselors' beds, shoes, and cubbies. These bugs eventually appeared in the dining hall hidden in a napkin or on the edge of a plate. It seemed to be a game where the finder would re-hide the bug in a new location. They showed up all over camp in the most unusual places. Nobody learned where all the bugs originally came from. And I have been grateful for that ever since!

Preparation

To prepare for participation in the marathons, I walked a minimum of five miles three to four times a week.

When I walked alone, Herm would drop me off at the beautiful and historic Valley Forge Park. He also picked me up when I was finished. This is the same historic place that General George Washington and his troops camped in 1776.

I followed a five-mile circular path of gentle hills with beautiful surroundings. Even I couldn't get lost; just follow the sidewalk. I often saw deer, squirrels, rabbits, and, occasionally, a fox. This path is very popular with dog walkers. It was generally quite pleasant to be out in the fresh air listening to the songs of the many different types of birds.

It was comforting to know as I came up over the hill and saw the Washington Memorial Chapel, the large Gothic Revival style church on the left side of the road, that it was time to call home. That way Herm and I would both arrive at the parking lot at the same time. The Eisenhower family used to attend this church. It is presently an active Episcopal church.

Many times my friends Gisela and Emily would walk with me. The three of us had been neighbors, friends, and walking buddies for many years. All I ever carried on my walks was a bottle of water and my cell phone. There were clean bathrooms all along the way, so I could drink as much as I needed to without worrying.

The three-day Philadelphia walk raised over six million dollars. I was personally responsible for $4,800. I'm proud to add that I raised twice what was required to enroll in this fundraiser. I'm equally proud that I was able to walk the sixty miles in three days with over 2,000 other participants, many of them cancer survivors.

Zora wearing her 3 day 60 mile walk tee shirt.

I have many wonderful memories from those three days. It began with Opening Ceremonies at Sesame Place in Langhorne, PA, a suburb of Philadelphia. As we began our adventure we received a pat on the back and a big wave from Elmo and Cookie Monster. It was here that I bumped into the daughter of a friend of mine and her two friends. It was the sound of her unique laughter that caught my attention in this monstrous crowd. They became my companions throughout the three-day walk. What a fortuitous encounter that turned out to be. Had I been walking on my own, I probably would have wandered off course more than once!

Two of the women were power walkers. I amazed myself by being able to keep up with them. Though it wasn't a race, we walked at a healthy pace. At the first pit stop, kids from Maple Point Middle School came out to show their support by serenading us with some popular tunes.

The route wound through cornfields into beautiful Core Creek Park. Some lovely ladies in pink wigs cheered us on in historic Newtown. After a luau lunch and one seriously steep incline, we ended the twenty-three-mile day on an old landing strip at Warminster Community Park. This was the longest day, the hottest day, and the most humid. I must admit I felt exhausted. All my muscles were screaming at me.

The location of the evening campsite was a tightly held secret because hundreds of women would be sleeping in tents without individual security. We needed to know because I planned to sleep at home in my own bed and Herm to pick me up. We were told of the location as late in the day as practical. I discovered other women chose to sleep in nearby hotels or at friends' homes. We all wanted a comfortable bed and a hot shower or bath. Moreover, having to wait in line by the rows of port-a-potties was hardly an appealing option. Finding my tent that would be identical to all the others in the middle of the night after using the port-a-potty would have proven to be a mammoth sleep disrupting complication.

Herm picked me up and ferried my sixty-five-year-old body back to our home. I immediately headed to our Jacuzzi, soaked in a soothing aromatic, bubble bath, had a quick bite to eat, and was asleep by 7:30 p.m.

After nearly a twelve-hour-night's rest, I arrived early and refreshed for day two. I met up with my walking buddies who had spent the night sleeping in the tents provided. Judging from their initial movements, I determined that I had had a far more relaxing and rejuvenating night.

The scenery on our second day included rural sites, a farm, and suburban neighborhoods. During our several pit stops, we received snacks and drinks. The volunteers were friendly and clearly focused on hygiene. All edibles were well wrapped. There were rows of very clean Port-a-Potties and lots of anti-bacterial handy wipes.

Each stop also featured something to entertain us. We saw people dressed to reflect the "invasion of nerds" at lunch. We passed through the town of Ambler and saw the beautifully decorated front porches. We got love beads at one pit stop and felt the love (during a real wedding) at the next.

After nineteen miles of walking, we finally rolled into Camp 2 at Montgomery County Community College. The day had been chilly in the early morning and pleasantly sunny the rest of the day. Knowing that I had completed two-thirds of the walk, I was feeling surprisingly good, in spite of developing blisters on my feet. I was definitely on a walker's high.

Day Three started with a twenty-five-mile bus ride at the base of one of the windiest, steepest hills of the walk. Yikes! After that long climb, we were rewarded with some great window-shopping in downtown Chestnut Hill. Following an even bigger and steeper hill, we walked down what is known as the Manayunk Bikers' Wall.

I was nearly euphoric. Walking downhill is much easier than going up. Also I was in step and keeping pace with my younger companions. Two of these young women were power walkers as I have previously mentioned. This really fed my ego. Our varied conversations kept pace with our gait. The spectators on the sidelines cheered us on with encouraging words, signs and music.

We were rewarded again with cheers and candy from residents of downtown Manayunk. After some entertainment by local clowns at lunch, we traveled along the peaceful Schuylkill River. The journey finally ended at the largest Park in Philadelphia –Fairmount Park—where we were greeted by friends, family and the entire Three-Day community. The closing ceremonies at the Mann Music Center were beautiful and exhilarating. Thanks to cell phones, Herm and I managed to find each other in this enormous crowd and headed home.

Another walking challenge that I set up for myself during this year was participating in The More Marathon. This marathon was created by the editors of *More* magazine and is designed for women over forty. I definitely met that requirement. Held in New York City, it is a 13.1-mile walk—twice around Central Park. I did this walk twice within twelve months. The first time I walked it shortly before my sixty-fifth birthday, and the second time was the day before my sixty-sixth birthday. Each time, Gisele and Emily did the More Marathon with me. The first year my sister-in-law Amy walked with us. The second year, my sister-in-law Faye joined us.

This was also the day of the large birthday celebration and party I had arranged for myself at the famous Tavern on the Green Restaurant in Central Park. The timing was perfect. I had invited a few dozen friends and relatives and was elated when everyone was able to attend, even friends from Israel.

The logistics for the four of us who had completed the marathon were quite amusing. We were not the only people planning to attend a celebration at The Tavern after completing the walk. We entered the restaurant dressed in our marathon walking attire, plastered down sweaty hair, and sweat socks, and sneakers. Sweatiness can't be over-emphasized.

Our plan of changing clothes in the ladies room was most definitely not unique to us. As we entered, we discovered that it was quite crowded and a bit redolent. We all laughed at ourselves as we shed the less pleasantly smelling clothing and attempted to wash up a bit before putting on our crumpled party dresses and heels.

We managed to brush our hair, apply some make-up, and hide our aches and pains as we walked over to the crowd awaiting our arrival.

It was a fabulous, memorable afternoon with lots of good food, drink, fun conversation, and laughter. I received the recognition I had been craving. It was a perfect way to complete the year of challenges with this celebration.

Swimming, a life-long passion, was a second area of physical prowess I decided to pursue. In January of my sixty-fifth year, I competed in the South Florida Senior Games. I entered four different competitions. In the 100-meter freestyle, I won the silver medal. In the 200-meter freestyle, I won the gold medal. I also took gold in the 100-meter breaststroke and silver in the 200-meter breaststroke. Just smile and call me Esther Williams!

Zora winning four Senior Olympics swimming medals.

I believe it's very fortunate that buttons aren't normally part of women's bathing suits because I was busting my buttons that day! Admittedly, I did select areas where the odds of doing well were in my favor. Swimming and long-distance walking required only physical effort.

Skiing

However, that was not the case with my accomplishment in Snowmass, Colorado, where I successfully skied the black diamond slopes.

Sitting in the chairlift going up the mountain led me to imagine myself as a bird flying with wings spread wide. Above me the sun was shining, and the snow way below me was bright, white, and sparkly. Standing at the top of the slope with my ski instructor, I listened to his directions on how to traverse the mountain's steep slope and avoid the moguls. His tall, slender build and dark ski outfit stood out, so he was easy to follow as he tacked like a sailboat making wide arcs in the snow as we descended the steep incline.

Bundled in long underwear beneath my stylish one-piece, zippered-front ski outfit with my matching knit ski hat covering my head and ears, I was eagerly anticipating succeeding at my last, and most difficult, physical challenge. Although I was wearing sunglasses under my dark ski goggles, my surroundings still seemed too bright and too white. I was squinting so hard to block the brightness, my eyes were hurting.

As we took off skiing parallel to the mountain, I was upright and feeling confident. We turned and headed slightly downward. My legs tightened, and my hands clenched my poles. My parallel skis opened into a wide snowplow. I finished that first turn standing upright and I started slowly breathing more naturally again. And with each successfully completed turn, I became more confident, upright and gradually able to increase my speed. We sashayed rhythmically down the slope. What an exhilarating feeling! By the time we reached the bottom, I was laughing and smiling from ear to ear. I had done it! When I repeated the run, it was even more thrilling because the fear was gone.

My sixty-fifth year was further enhanced by my good fortune to be able to combine several of my passions and talents. The opportunity presented itself when I learned of the four-day Upledger sponsored course for Advanced CranioSacral Therapists (CST) in the Bahamas.

CranioSacral Therapy was developed by osteopathic physician John E. Upledger, DO. It is a hands-on modality that seeks to identify and release restrictions in the body's CranioSacral System. This system consists of the membranes and fluids that surround the brain and spinal cord and influences the body's self-correcting abilities.

When it is operating at optimal efficiency, the CranioSacral System can enhance the body's ability to detect the stresses and strains of daily life. Conversely, restrictions in the smooth operation of the system could cause sensory, motor, or neurological disabilities. These problems may include such things as chronic pain, vision difficulties, scoliosis, motor coordination impairment, learning disabilities, as well as other dysfunctions of the central nervous system.

CST is a very gentle, hands-on modality that looks and can feel similar to Reiki or Therapeutic Touch. The client can be sitting or lying on a massage table. The therapist places hands on various parts of the client's body to pick up the CranioSacral rhythm. This informs the therapist about areas of bodily distress. The client may feel little or only the movement of the therapist's hand from one location to another. The client may notice a change in breathing or a feeling of calm and relaxation. At times the therapist will have a dialogue with the client about what sensations or thoughts the client might be having. It is a gentle, non-invasive modality that works with both the physical and emotional aspects of the client's condition.

Dolphins

This course involved swimming with dolphins in the Bahamas in August while learning to utilize more of these techniques. I qualified to take this advanced training because I am a certified CranioSacral Therapist and a teaching assistant. The cherry on top of this delicious opportunity was that it was being taught by Dr. John Upledger, the CranioSacral guru himself.

A short time before the class was to begin, I received a letter from the Upledger Institute stating that Dr. John had fallen and injured his knee. As a consequence, he would not be teaching this class. His balance problem and the boat's motion were incompatible. I could take the class at a future date with Dr. John. The alternative was that his wife would fill in for him and teach this scheduled course. I had taken other classes with his wife and found her teaching style very compatible with my learning style. So I opted to move forward as scheduled.

Since this class was to take place in water for extensive periods, a wetsuit was a requirement. My son lent me his, which was rarely used and just hanging in his closet. When I was packing the wetsuit, Adam said to me, "Mom, you know what happens when you are in the water for many hours and you have to pee? You just do it!" I am not sure if he thought that he would gross me out or make me laugh. His comment did both.

I flew to the Bahamas, greatly anticipating this adventure. Though I am a good swimmer and not afraid of deep water, I knew for everyone's safety, I would have to let the class know on Day One about my limited vision. As I have already confessed, I have a difficult time telling strangers (actually anybody) about my visual limitations. Speaking about being legally blind (my life long secret) has always been a very emotional issue for me.

I effectively negotiated going through the airport and taking the taxi to our resort on my own. When I travel by myself, airports can be tricky. I felt extremely proud of myself and couldn't wait to tell Herman.

It seemed to be my lucky day. While registering for my room, I was able to upgrade from an efficiency, which provided a pull-out couch, to a roomette with a king-size bed, a couch, kitchen table, chairs, and a mini kitchen. The rooms were only a few steps from the dock where Upledger's boat, the *Dolphin Star*, was docked. A few of the women slept on the ship in bunk beds. They had very tight quarters, but that made lodging more cost effective.

As I was checking in, I met one of the women in the class. She showed me to the pool area where a few of the other women had gathered. We all introduced ourselves. We spoke about the various CranioSacral Therapy classes we had taken and our varied practices. I was the only physical therapist. The other women were massage or CranioSacral therapists.

It so happened that one of these women had been on the plane with me from Fort Lauderdale to Freeport, Bahamas. We bemoaned the fact that we weren't aware of the other's presence at the time. We could have shared a cab and conversation.

Dream

The night prior to the class I had a dream about Arthur Meyer standing on a long upward-moving escalator. Arthur was the camp director who hired me as a teenager at Camp HES (Hebrew Education Society). As I previously mentioned, the campers and counselors knew these initials stood for Happiness Every Summer.

Arthur was a kind, caring teacher who treated teenagers like adults. This was a quality that I found very rare in adults when I was a teenager. By this time, Arthur had been deceased for many years. I viewed this dream of him going up an escalator as a positive omen. I noted the dream in my journal but didn't write in detail about it or try to analyze it any further. I needed to sleep and be ready for the dolphin class in the morning.

On our first morning, we were given a tour of the ship. We were a group of ten women, ranging in age from forty to sixty-five, me being the oldest. The majority of the women were in their fifties. Two of the women were in their early sixties. Also aboard was the teacher, a teaching assistant, and the boat captain of Upledger's *Dolphin Star*.

After learning our way around, we sat in a circle at the stern of the sailboat to introduce ourselves to each other before the class officially began. I was somewhere in the middle of the circle. I kept telling myself these women were all professional CranioSacral Therapists and had seen and treated all sorts of disabilities. I thought this might make me feel less on edge. It didn't.

After sharing a very brief bio, I softly whispered, "I don't have good distance vision, so if the ship moves away or other ships are close by, please keep an eye on me so I don't get lost." My insides were turning summersaults, and my body shook as I spoke that simple sentence.

But I kept my voice soft and controlled. It was the first time I ever had told a group of strangers about my vision. If I hadn't been concerned about everyone's safety in the water, I never would have mentioned it. I hoped that I would never have to admit that to anyone again, especially not a group of strangers. Nobody commented, but they all seemed to make a mental note of my statement. Did they realize how difficult it was for me to tell them that about myself? I didn't die, faint, or cry as I gave them that information. Fortunately, at no time did I have a problem, and to my relief, nobody asked for further details about my vision. I survived my first personal public admission of my vision deficit.

I have just relaxed my rigid, upright posture and exhaled the breath I was holding while writing the above paragraph. I am now releasing my fingers from its death held grip on the pen.

As I look back on my disclosure, I realize that their reaction was what I had initially expected and what I thought I wanted: Nobody said anything. However, I hadn't shared how secretive I've always been about my lack of visual acuity nor the highly emotional issue it has always been for me. The experience I was going through at that moment was monumental for me. To them, it must have seemed like just another physical shortcoming that they were being told about. And while this was what I had expected, I was enormously disappointed that they didn't compliment me on the huge emotional challenge I had just surmounted. My anxiety level prior to and during my revelation was one of the highest I've ever experienced. So it took me quite a while before I realized the irony of my huge emotional investment and the minor impact on my listeners.

Our first activity was to swim with the dolphins in the canal. The dolphins seemed playful and not afraid of us. They were good at the game of "monkey see, monkey do."

If we swam in a circle, they swam a circle around us. If we dove up and down, they followed. In spite of their size, they moved though the water with ease and grace. One dolphin liked to swim next to me and rub up against me. Her touch felt like friendly communication similar to a warm handshake or hug. When the dolphin and I made eye contact, something wonderful happened. I felt a sensation of ease, calm, and peace spread throughout my body. Everything inside me and surrounding me felt light, expansive, and blissful. It was as though the dolphin was reading me and sending me her benevolence. The other women reported similar experiences.

One of the dolphins our group worked with was the first male born in captivity. My CranioSacral session as the client was with a female dolphin, also born in captivity. At one point, I was comfortably floating on my back encircled by three of my classmates. Their hands were strategically placed on my body to pick up my CranioSacral rhythm and to connect with each other. To me this session felt similar to having a session on a massage table. The extra benefits here included the bright sun warming me, the gentle waves rocking me, and a soft breeze of salt sea air engulfing me.

I was feeling calm and relaxed in this environment until my head bumped into a hard object. I thought I hit the edge of the dock. But no, it was the rostrum of the dolphin connecting with my skull. She then gently touched the various bones of my skull with her head. As she swam underneath and encircled me the water rippled and made waves that gently rocked my body. She would connect by touching different areas of my body where I had had a pain or weakness. She kept returning to my occipital bone, the bottom back of my skull. Behind this bone is the area where the visual system resides. Obviously, this is my area of weakness.

When she swam under me, I felt light and airy. As she touched the trunk of my body, it felt as though club soda was bubbling through me. Perhaps this was a sonar connection. Echolocation is a process that allows dolphins to emit sound waves that hit an object and are bounced back, allowing them to identify the location, shape, and size of the objects. Dolphins need echolocation to navigate, locate prey, hunt, and protect themselves from predators.

At any rate, it was an extremely pleasant, enlightening, and healing sensation. I could feel my body breathe, expand, lighten, and relax.

Many dolphin therapy programs work with the physically and emotionally disabled, autism, and returning military personal. Dolphin therapy has been shown to decrease stress and related symptoms. Participants experience improved motivation, attention span, gross and fine motor skills, physical strength, communication, and social interaction.

We had a long break for lunch that first day, so we students took two cabs into town for lunch, sightseeing, and shopping. Some of the women bought typical island souvenirs. I purchased a small, clear glass dolphin standing on its tail as a remembrance of this adventure. I keep it in Florida next to my collection of mermaids. I only possess two dolphins, so it is not considered a collection.

Dolphins are considered aquatic mammals because they nurse their offspring and breathe through their lungs. Shortly after they are born, mothers bring their offspring up to the water surface for their first breath. Throughout their lives, they frequently come to the surface to breathe air. Dolphins use echolocation to navigate and hunt. They travel in pods and can grow to be eight feet long and live to be forty to sixty years old. They live in temperate tropical waters. Bottlenecks are the most common species. Sailors view dolphins as good luck because they have been known to save people from drowning.

Returning from our lunch break, we got back into our wet and cold wetsuits. Once in the water, we warmed up quickly. We needed to wear them to maintain our body temperature and protect us from the tropical sun. I did use a lot of suntan lotion on my face, neck, hands and feet. I also wore dark swimming goggles. Sunglasses were useless in the water.

Our boat, the *Dolphin Star*, took us to a lovely secluded beach where the water was shallow enough for us to stand and the waves were gentle. We worked in small groups of three or four. One person was treated to a CranioSacral session by the other therapists in the group. Here we worked with each other without any dolphins. Most of us believed that even though dolphins were not physically present, we were able to call upon their energy to assist us in our process.

The essence of my session was that now that I am a senior, elder, wise woman, crone, it is time for me to believe wholly and completely in my own know-how and capabilities. Time for me to accept being legally blind and not let that hold me back any longer. I can honor myself for all that I have accomplished up to this point.

This is the same message I received from Arthur Meyer in my dream. He believed in me when I was seventeen. Now that I have become a senior citizen, he helped me see myself as even more capable, accomplished and competent. I have made a practice of paying attention to my dreams and let them guide me.

Water has always been an element that I have enjoyed and felt at ease in. As a child I loved my bath, splashing as I played with boats and rubber ducks in the tub. At summer camp, I quickly learned how to swim and dive. I easily passed the American Red

Cross swimming tests. When I completed the junior life saving test, I decided that I had gone as far as I needed to. Water feels like home to me.

I enjoy water for drinking, bathing, swimming, exercising, socializing, and meditating in. It is an integral part of my life.

Mikvah

Therefore, it is not surprising that the other water activity during my sixty-fifth year was a religious ceremony — entering the mikvah. I performed this ritual the Friday before I read from the Torah in my synagogue.

The mikvah is a Jewish ritual bath used individually by men before the Sabbath and women after menstruation for spiritual purification. I decided to create a rebirthing ceremony for myself and used the time to honor the special women in my life. My friend Iris came with me as my witness and helper.

We made an altar by covering a bench with a beautiful silk scarf. I placed symbols of the other elements of life: earth (a stone), fire (my grandmother's brass Shabbat candle sticks), and air (a blown-up balloon). On the corner of the table was an antique candlestick telephone for communication, my personal symbol. There were three framed photographs (Mom, Grandma Erna, and

Louise) on the table in front of a vase of beautiful red roses, my favorite flower.

Before entering the water, I spoke from my heart to the picture of each of these three women thanking them for their love, nurturing, and guidance. I felt the spirits of these endearing mothers surround me with love and approval. I then disrobed and walked naked down the steps into the warm water. I recited the ritual prayers and performed the required total body submerging. In the warm water I felt buoyant, expanded in space and time and appreciated for who I have become.

Reading Torah

The following day I read from the Torah at my synagogue. My preparation had taken the better part of a year. Reading *Haftorah* at Congregation Or Shalom, of which my husband and I are founding members, posed a number of challenges for me.

My singing voice is less than melodious, and chanting is required as one reads the Hebrew words of biblical passages. My friend Jerry tutored me and made me a cassette tape of my portion to listen to and sing along with. I practiced diligently while doing my daily morning walk around Valley Forge Park. My mother would have been proud of me for using my time efficiently!

Sometimes I feared what people passing by me thought of a middle-aged woman walking along at a rapid clip mumbling to herself in a foreign language with lots of guttural sounds. Curiously, no one stopped to ask me if I was okay.

The book that I practiced reading my portion from was published by the Jewish Braille Institute of America, Inc. The Hebrew print was large, black, and bold on a white nine-by-twelve-inch page. The Torah doesn't include vowels, but this text did because it was a learning tool. Hebrew vowels are small dots and dashes usually under the consonants.

When I read with or without glasses I need to hold what I am reading close to my face. I call it smelling my book. This became a big problem for me with the Torah lying flat on the lectern. Therefore, the top lines in the Torah are farther away from my eyes than the bottom lines. I couldn't get physically close enough to the top lines to read them when the Torah was lying flat even if I bent over it. Doing that kind of bending didn't look graceful or feel comfortable. So Handy Herman built a slanted lectern to sit on top of the existing flat one.

This angled the Torah toward me in a more upright position. Thus, the upper words were closer to me. This solved one problem but caused another. I wasn't tall enough even with my thin, high-heeled shoes to see the top lines. So I was given the small slotted step used by short Bar and Bat Mitzvah students to give them height to see over the lectern.

Thus, I gingerly stepped up to read from the top of the Torah column and down as I recited the words on the lower part. This dance added exercise to my recitation. On my second step down, my left high heel got caught in the open slat of the step. I had to step out of the shoe as I couldn't wiggle it out of the narrow opening. Thus, I was standing on the Bimah with one shoe off like, "Diddle, diddle dumpling, my son John. One shoe off and one shoe on."

As I read from the different Hebrew columns, I continued to step up and down, feeling very off balanced and lopsided. Before I sat down, one of the men on the Bimah yanked my high heel shoe out of the step's slat so I could walk away from behind the lectern. This shoe glitch became a laughing matter later as part of "the highs and lows" of my recitation.

Having completed this challenge permitted me to demonstrate that I could overcome my fears and limitations. Standing before a large crowd and chanting

Hebrew which I could barely see was as far from the little girl who tried desperately to remain unseen as I could possibly get.

Locks of Love

During this celebratory year, I cut my beautiful, long, wavy brown hair. Since I was thinking and acting differently, I wanted a different appearance.

I gave my cut hair to Locks of Love. Locks of Love makes wigs for cancer patients from donated hair. Added to this donation was saved hair that had been cut at ages sixteen, twenty-one, thirty and sixty-five.

Herm and I also celebrated many non-challenging special events together that year, including our sixty-fifth birthdays and our forty-fourth anniversary. We made sure to visit all our grandchildren for their birthdays and celebrated with cake and ice cream. We enjoyed the warmth of Florida from December through February in our Hallendale apartment. We visited our son Adam in March to celebrate his birthday and ski at Mount Sunapee in New Hampshire where he was a ski instructor. In August we enjoyed a two-week Baltic cruise with good friends.

For me, this year was a major turning point in how I saw myself. I accomplished everything I set out to do. I stopped thinking of myself as a slacker. Being legally blind was no longer a secret nor an impediment to my overcoming obstacles.

I also had many ceremonies with healing groups I belonged to. I was treated to many delicious birthday lunches and dinners with friends at restaurants or in their homes. I made a birthday book in which my friends wrote me notes of love, advice, humor, and birthday wishes. I treasure it and reread it whenever I feel the need to cheer myself up or recall the feelings of achievement and satisfaction I experienced in 2005.

Everything I set out to do that year I accomplished! It was a wonderful year of physical, mental, emotional, educational, and religious challenges. I only wish my parents could have been there. Mom would have been most proud of my swimming and Dad of my walking. I felt Grandma Erna's presence with me all the way, especially when I was on the Bimah reading from the Torah. This year proved to me that anything I put my mind to do I could do successfully!

Walking
- Three-day 60 Mile Philadelphia Breast Cancer Walk
    - Day 1: 23 miles
    - Day 2: 19 miles
    - Day 3: 22 miles
- More Marathon—13.1 miles (twice around Central Park in New York)
    - On my sixty-fifth birthday
    - On my sixty-sixth birthday, I beat my previous time by fifteen minutes.

Swimming
- South Florida Senior Games - Swimming
    - 100 meter freestyle—silver medal
    - 200 meter freestyle—gold medal
    - 100 meter breaststroke—gold medal
    - 200 meter breaststroke—silver medal

Skiing
- Snowmass, Colorado—I skied the black diamond slopes.

Physical
- I lost forty-two pounds

Educational
- Swimming and doing CranioSacral Therapy with the dolphins in the Bahamas

Religious
- *Mikvah*—ritual bath
- Reading Torah

Family
- Celebrating our forty-fourth anniversary and our sixty-fifth birthdays; Zora, March 27 and Herman, April 5
- Visited our grandchildren on their birthdays
- Large holiday dinners at our home, for Rosh Ha Shana and Passover

Donations
- Breast cancer research: $4,800
- Locks of Love: I gave my very long hair which I had cut and saved at ages sixteen, twenty-one, thirty, and sixty-five.

Celebrations

- A Baltic Cruise with friends
- Many luncheons, dinners, and parties with friends and family

The feeling of success is a wonderful high. Wouldn't you like to have that feeling?

What is your challenge?

A challenge is that thing that you find difficult and stimulating simultaneously. It is that thing you have been meaning to do forever but somehow never make the time or space to do it. **So Do It Now!**

Action Exercise

1. Name your challenge.
2. What is your motivation and potential goal?
3. Establish a time frame.
4. Write out how you will know when you have reached you goal.
5. Celebrate your accomplishment.

Helpful hints:

1. Write out your challenge on a three-by-five card. Then place this card on your bathroom mirror, desk, and kitchen table.
2. Read it often.
3. Tell friends about your challenge, so they can support you.
4. Keep a journal to record your progress.

Let me know how you are doing. Contact me at zorapt@email.com

CHAPTER 12

Flying Solo

I am guided by inner wisdom.

W hen traveling to unfamiliar places, I am more comfortable being with another person who has a more complete view of the landscape. I am a follower, not a leader in that situation. But if push comes to shove, I can and have done it by myself. This chapter is not strictly about airplanes and airports. It's about my ability to be independent while traveling in unfamiliar places alone. So, I've aptly titled this chapter Flying Solo.

Prior to my very first flight, the only information I had about flying I learned from the humorous anecdotes my father had shared when I was a child. My father's first flights took place when he was in the army during WWI. He would describe the inside of an airplane as being a deep, dark, metal cavern held together by rusty nuts, bolts, and wads of chewing gum. He talked about the bumpy rides and the loop-de-loops the pilots created to see how many soldiers they could make upchuck. I'm sure my Dad was one of them, though this he didn't disclose, and I was wise enough not to ask. My father's facial expressions and hand gestures would have me giggling as he wove the fabric of his tall tale.

At the age of twenty-seven, I took my first airplane trip. Herman walked me to the gate and kissed me goodbye. I showed my ticket and walked onto the plane alone. Shock of shocks! I found the interior of this plane modern and clean. No rusty screws, bolts, or chewing gum visible anywhere. I found my seat by the window and buckled up. At this time, I was nearly eight months pregnant with my second child. I carried small; nevertheless, I made sure to wear a large, plaid cape to hide my protruding belly. I was president of the local ORT chapter, and I was now heading to the National Women's American ORT Convention for a week.

Organization for Rehabilitation through Training (ORT) began in Russia in 1880. Its purpose was to promote vocational training for skilled labor and farming for impoverished Jews. These schools were started by men for men and spread throughout Europe and America in the early 1920s.

In 1927, the wives of the original officers organized the Women's American ORT. Today, in addition to the original focus, the training has expanded to include both men and women in a variety of training programs and workshops. The organization's active fundraising provides scholarships, apprenticeships, social and recreational activities.

When I shared my plans of flying for the first time to the ORT convention, my friend suggested that it was best not to eat before flying. The airline would be serving lunch on the plane. I heeded this advice and was famished by the time lunch came. I gobbled it down. A short time later, we hit some air turbulence. I hastily found the appropriate paper bag and wretchedly gave back my lunch. This left me alternately perspiring or having chills. This was far from the pleasant flight I anticipated.

Luggage

With no more mishaps aboard the aircraft, we landed safely, and I found the ORT group. Everyone was collecting luggage from the carousel. My luggage wasn't among the rest. I happened to glance up at an overhead conveyor belt carrying luggage in the sky. There was my black suitcase decorated with large white adhesive taped Z's. As it slowly moved away, I pointed and yelled "There's my bag up there! There's my suitcase!" Nobody did a thing! My luggage wasn't found when we boarded our bus to the hotel. I was assured that it would be sent to our hotel directly. Apparently, "directly" meant two and a half days because that was when I next laid eyes on it!

I shared a room with three other young women. Nobody had maternity clothes. I washed my underwear and blouse at night and the women formed a circle with their hair dryers and blew them dry. Thus, I could put them back on the next morning. One *zaphtic* (chubby) lady at the conference lent me a T-shirt and a blouse. So I had something to sleep in and something else to wear to meetings. The hotel supplied me with toiletries. All the women mothered me. Luckily, I wasn't one of the speakers.

I spent two and a half days calling the airport before my suitcase appeared. I never did find out what happened, but I was seriously relieved to change into my maternity clothes. This, my first flight, was probably the worst experience I ever had flying. Be prepared, the Girl Scout motto, is the lesson this flight taught me. Now when I fly with Herman, I put underwear and an outfit in his suitcase, just in case. He does the same with my suitcase.

Fast forward to April 2017, when I attended a writing retreat in Costa Rica. I knew no one who was going, and I had never met Christine Kloser who was leading the workshop. I had been following a writing program of Christine's online and thought highly of her abilities. Among many other things, this young woman is an entrepreneur, author, and transformational author's coach.

My book, which I started before this workshop, tells my story of feeling unqualified and unworthy because of a birth defect. This limitation caused me to feel like an outsider and failure. However, it has been through my sense of failures that I have learned and have grown into an accomplished and accepting senior citizen. I like David Bowie's summary of this situation. "Aging is an extraordinary process where you become the person you should always have been."

As I explain elsewhere in this memoir, my dream is to become a *New York Times* bestselling author. Mine is a transformational story. I have changed my self-image and beliefs. I now can see and credit myself for the things I have accomplished in spite of my severe visual disability. For me, the cup is always half full. I hope that others can profit from lessons my experiences have provided. If I can inspire even one person to replace a negative self-image with a positive one, then this effort will have been worthwhile.

Airports

Even though the West Palm and Fort Lauderdale airports are closer to my Florida home, I took a direct flight to Costa Rica from the Miami airport to obviate the need for changing planes. My level of independence doesn't need to be made unnecessarily more difficult.

Once again, Herman dropped me off in front of my airline for me to fly solo. And, yes, he kissed me goodbye this time too. With my luggage, passport, and boarding pass in hand, I confidently walked in and marched directly up to the luggage/ticket line. There I deposited my large gray suitcase decorated with two colorful woolen pompons around the handle and white adhesive taped Z's on the top and front. Again the decorations were to help me spot my luggage when I had to retrieve it at my destination. I would be alone with no one else to see and grab it for me. I paid the requisite luggage fee (this clearly was not 1967) and headed to my departure gate.

Of course, flying in 2017 requires first going through security. The line snaked around slowly but continually moved. When I reached the security guard, I handed him my passport and boarding pass. As instructed, I raised my sunglasses for him to see my eyes. He noticed it was a new passport and that I hadn't yet signed it. In the passport picture I had short hair. My hair is long now. I told him my husband picked the picture. He kept looking down at the picture and then back at me. My vivid imagination transported me into the pages of novels with characters being detained and thrown into jail on bogus charges. After what seemed like an eternity, he handed back my passport. It was then that I realized I had been literally holding my breath.

To me the security checks seemed very lax. Laptop computers did not have to be uncased. No one had to remove their shoes. I found this lack of vigilance disappointing. Because of my age, I no longer need to remove my shoes. I enjoy having the guard point at my feet saying, "Miss, take off your shoes." I smile and ask if he would like to see my ID. This always makes me feel good. They think that I look younger than my chronological age. What woman, in her right mind, wants to admit that she is seventy-five or older?

As I leave the security area, I ask someone in a uniform for directions to my gate. I ask a few more times as I walk down the twisting hallway to make sure I am heading in the right direction. I barely notice the fast food restaurants, bookstores, and T-shirt shops on either side of my path. Luckily the gate signs are very large. I can read them if I stand directly below them. When I finally arrived at the gate after the long walk, I asked the airline personnel if this was the gate for Costa Rica. She answered in the affirmative. I found a seat and then called Herm to tell him I had successfully made it to the gate and we would be taking off in a few minutes. I now finally breathed easily.

The announcement came that my flight number was boarding for Liberia. Oh no! I wasn't going to Africa! I was supposed to be going to Costa Rica. I turned to the woman seated next to me who seemed totally composed and not at all rattled by this announcement and asked her if this plane was going to Costa Rica. She said, "Yes, Liberia is the name of the airport." Once again, I exhaled my held breath.

For an international trip, this plane seemed quite small, and it was full. There was space in the overhead for my computer suitcase. The three-hour ride was going well until the flight attendants handed out the immigration forms. Herm usually filled these out when we traveled together. The forms are small enough to fit inside a passport. As a consequence, the print is minuscule. I couldn't see well enough to read any of it even wearing my reading glasses and using a magnifying glass. I finally asked the young lady sitting next to me to please read the questions to me because I couldn't see them. She was sweet and obliging. She even acknowledged that she found the print very small.

Having to ask for help from a total stranger brought me back to my childhood when I wasn't allowed to cross the street by myself. We lived in a high traffic area with wide streets. I usually looked for a woman who also was waiting for the traffic light to change to ask if she would hold my hand as we crossed a busy Brooklyn street. Nobody ever refused me. Most of the women would smile sweetly at me.

Isn't it funny now when I need help I ask younger women who are just as kind and caring? I find it's a rare occasion when a stranger won't provide help to someone who needs a simple favor. I believe that as a species we really do recognize that we're all in this together.

Deplaning in the Liberia airport, I had my passport and immigration papers in hand and followed the crowd. I am a good follower as a result of lots of practice. When it was my turn at the immigration booth, I complained about the small size of the print. The man behind the desk said that he had heard that complaint many times before as he handed back my passport.

I easily retrieved my decorated luggage from the circular moving conveyor belt. Then I followed the crowd to the exit. As I reached the door to go outside, there were many people holding signs, none of which I could read. It wasn't because they were written in Spanish. I was just unable to decipher the small print. When I asked for my travel group, a man stepped forward, took my large luggage, and said in accented English, "Follow me."

I trailed after him as he walked outside into the bright sunshine. We strolled past many groups of people standing or sitting by the curbside. Finally, he brought me to my group and pulled a plastic chair up to the table for me to join the assembled group of six; two men and four women. We needed to wait for two more arrivals before we could board our van which would transport us to our resort.

It seemed that the people who were waiting all knew each other. They had been together at a previous writing workshop in York, PA. Wow! That would have been way more convenient for me since it's less than two hours from my home in King of Prussia.

I introduced myself by my name and self-anointed title, Queen of King of Prussia. This got its usual laugh. With an unusual name and a title people tend to remember me. I did announce that I was writing a memoir which will include one of my main themes: "dis the dis in disability."

To switch the focus of attention away from myself, I asked them to introduce themselves to me. I learned a little about each of them. All of them were from the United States from all walks of life with ages ranging from the forties to the seventies.

Sitting and baking in the scorching sun required us to drink a lot of water. I went with two of the women into the gift shop to purchase bottled water for the hour and a half it would take us to drive to the resort. I was shocked to find that a 16-ounce bottle of water was so expensive. Feeling that I had been a victim of highway robbery, my writing retreat adventure began.

Our van trip involved going up a narrow, windy, mountainous road that seemed to go on for miles and miles. The lively conversation begun at the airport came to a sudden halt when the driver advised us the van had Wi-Fi. At that moment, virtually everyone else became glued to their cell phones or iPads just like a bunch of teenagers. The driver also told us that the air conditioning was on high but we hardy felt it. It was humid and close inside the van.

The woman sitting next to me was clearly not feeling well. Prior to our journey, she had been very talkative and animated. In the van she looked shrunken, pale, and lost her gift of gab. She confided that the ride was making her feel car sick. I gave her some Tums to help settle her stomach. She dozed and so did I. We awoke when we stopped at a grocery store to pick up supplies and snacks for the week since our resort was in a remote area.

The Resort

We were all happy to leave the stuffy van when we reached our destination. We got a warm welcome from the hotel staff who took the luggage to our rooms.

The resort was rustic but lovely. The ocean and beach were in front of us. Behind us was a wooded area where our rooms were located. The iguanas, geckos, crabs, colorful song birds, and howling monkeys were easily visible. Each morning I engaged in an hour-long yoga class held on a raised wooden gazebo facing the ocean. The rolling waves in front of us and the symphony of birdsongs from around us provided for an enhanced yoga experience and a tranquil beginning to our workday.

Our three meals each day were always appetizing, delicious, and healthy. The providers made sure to take into account the specific culinary needs of the participants (vegan, food allergies, gluten or dairy free). Wonderful blended fresh fruit drinks of papaya, mango, pineapple, and other fruits were served with each meal.

But the best parts of meals were the conversations and learning about one another. Conversations were inclusive, enthusiastic, and varied. We talked about books we had read, books we were writing, our families, our homes, our interests, and our worries. At the end of nearly all meals, we lingered to continue our conversations. On some occasions, we may have lingered longer as a means of delaying getting back to writing. At least that was true in my case.

The Retreat

Each morning after breakfast we had a group meeting in the gazebo where we got to check in with each other. At the end of the meeting each of us told the group what our intention for the day was. I found that sharing mine with the group was exceedingly valuable in encouraging me to stay true to my plan.

The purpose of this retreat week wasn't to teach us how to write but to provide us with an enchanting environment in which to write. We were far away from the daily demands and worries of home, family, school, or work. Except for our pre-breakfast mandatory meeting, the day was ours to do with as we wished. Should we need it, there was technical and spiritual support readily available from the facilitators. There even was a massage therapist on the premises.

Some people set up their laptops on tables in the gazebo facing the ocean. They enjoyed the music of the waves lapping against the shore. Also the gentle breeze blowing through the open gazebo kept them cool. The sun lovers slathered themselves in suntan lotion and headed to the beach to sit on a towel or in a lounge chair. They wrote by hand in a journal or used an iPad. I was amused to see one man just snoozing in the sun. Our daily schedule was of our own making.

My Hideaway

I found an isolated table on the porch off the dining room. I set up my laptop, which I had not been using at home. I put on my new eSight glasses. I was new at using both the laptop and these glasses, I was not accustomed to adjusting the multiple buttons and knobs for power, zoom, distance, focus, contrast, home, panning, menu, and menu return. I was self-conscious about being seen wearing them. They made me look like I came from outer space. The glasses needed to be plugged into the laptop. It seemed like it took forever just to set up. I wanted to be by myself, unobserved. Also when (not if) technical help was needed, our conversation wouldn't disturb anyone else.

The computer guru, a woman from Pennsylvania, spent a lot of time helping me set up my laptop (print size, contrast, font, a visible mouse icon, and such). She could discern what I needed before I even mentioned the issue. She clearly explained the technology to me in terms that I could follow and comprehend easily. That alone made the trip extremely valuable to me. She genuinely understood my visual limitations and made the necessary accommodations on the computer for me. She was a great comfort to me, alleviating much of my angst and frustration. I affectionately called her "My New Herm." When I have a computer problem at home, I automatically call out "Herm," and he good-naturedly comes to my rescue—even though he sometimes expresses his belief that "Herm" is just another four-letter word!

"My New Herm" is a tall, solidly built, short-haired, intelligent, open-hearted woman who giggles easily and offers warm, encouraging hugs. She enjoyed the nickname I bestowed upon her. She referred to herself that way frequently during the week. Her kind words reassured me that these technical glitches would disappear, and then composing words would be all I'd need to focus on. I fretted over having lost the first three days of my writing time due to technical difficulties.

Time Management

From the morning discussions, it became apparent that many of us were having issues with managing our time as effectively as we wished. The only scheduled events were yoga (which was optional), the nine a.m. get together and mealtimes. The rest of the day was ours to do with it as we pleased. One woman let time slip by while she enjoyed the sun, surf, sand, and conversation rather than writing. The woman who had been carsick in our van spent the first three days sleeping and working through a deeply troubling emotional issue. I thought about the man I had spotted taking a siesta in the afternoon sun.

These and similar examples helped me to realize that the side roads, detours, and annoyances we experience while traveling on our individual writing journeys are an essential part of the route. I recognized that the fare required to make the trip is learning to demonstrate greater patience—both with ourselves and others.

The workshop leaders made themselves totally accessible to us. Their coaching included more than just helping with the actual words on the page. Their individualized attention provided us with whatever kind of support we needed. For some, it was clearly emotional support. For others, it was help with structuring their time. In my case, I needed help with setting up and using my equipment. In addition, I truly welcomed the emotional support as well.

I was brought up strictly observing our number one family rule: We never disclosed a personal problem or issue outside of the immediate family. I was cautioned to never talk about such things as the age of adult family members or their personal finances. Such topics were totally taboo. Medical problems and other family issues were a couple of the skeletons we kept firmly locked in the closet.

Help from a Special Teacher

Mrs. Watkins, my fourth-grade teacher, sparked my interest in history when she taught about the Greek and Roman empires. I could feel her passion for this subject.

Mythology and the dynamic personalities of the gods and goddesses enthralled me. The Greek and Roman gods seemed to have the same titles and roles, but their names were different. Zeus was the Greek king and Jupiter was Roman. Each had families, and like all families, they had squabbles. The gods appealed to my imagination. They tended to be heroes who for the most part fought off evil and prevented chaos. On the other hand, like humans, they were not perfect or always good. They too had failings and foibles.

As a child, I could find ways to relate to different types of personalities. If I found this easy, why couldn't my teachers understand my shy personality and learn how to relate to me? Because of my skill and interest in relating to others, it's not surprising that I majored in psychology in college.

My appreciation for the way Mrs. Watkins approached teaching encouraged my parents to hire her as a tutor for me. She was the only tutor that I ever accepted. During the summers, Mom drove me to her home—a lovely, old brownstone townhouse in Brooklyn Heights—for lessons. She made learning fun with games and puzzles. During the summer she prepared me for the next year's curriculum, especially in the subjects where there would be a lot of reading.

Her large patio overlooked the beautiful and busy East River. She would point out the different types of boats as they floated by: ferries, schooners, tugs, sloops, and cargo ships. I never saw the fishing boats. I only heard about them because they came out early in the mornings and took their catch directly to the Fulton Fish Market which was known for having the freshest fish in Brooklyn. Jews frequented it on Thursdays and Catholics on Fridays. Our family usually had fish on Thursday nights for dinner. Louise made a delicious baked salmon or salmon croquets.

When it came to grades at school, my parents weren't the typical Jewish parents. For me learning content was more important than the marks I received. However, my older brother was expected to get good grades because he held the position of first-born son and grandson. Did he, you ask? Sorry, this is not a tell-all book.

My parents didn't expect any great academic achievement on my part. Mom read my assignments to me and made sure I wrote and handed in all my homework in elementary school. The teachers always passed me and sometimes wrote that I was improving or that I was a sweet, well-behaved little girl.

Now as a sometimes-jaded adult, I realize that the teachers had to pass me because my parents were paying tuition for a private school. My brother, my cousins, and all the children living in our apartment building went to private schools. Early mornings, we all congregated in front of our apartment house waiting for our different school buses. We would sometimes make bets on whose bus would be first or last just to have fun while waiting.

My inner child is driving me to write this book. She is now ready to make her voice heard. Here is some correspondence she and I shared at this spring writing retreat.

Letters

Dear Cookie,

I want to acknowledge all that you have done for me. I want you to know how deeply I love and appreciate you. I know and understand your pain and sorrow. I grieve for you.

I have moved on and left you behind. I am now coming back for you. I want you to continue on my journey with me. No more flying solo; I need you. You are my soul and my heart. You have fought many successful battles and won. Your spirit is enduring and endearing. I honor your strength and fortitude.

I, the adult Zora, am finally working on becoming whole. I need you with me. Will you be my support system? Will you become my cheerleader? Help us to see and acknowledge our loveliness, accomplishments, intellect, compassion, and fortitude.

We used to be friends that played and laughed together. This book will be a team effort because it is based on our life's experience.

Your older self,
Zora

Dear Zora,

I am afraid of change. I know who I am, a child with a visual disability. A good little girl who is sometimes seen but rarely heard. My role and behavior are ingrained in my essence. I have had no voice for so long I don't know how to speak up for myself. I take what is given me but ask for nothing more from the outside world. Due to my frustrations, I can be a holy terror at home with temper tantrums. However, I know that I am loved and fully accepted by all my family.

What you are asking of me will be very difficult. I don't like change! I fear being alone. But I love and honor you too. Help me, and I will try to be your cheerleader. Teach me to grow and change. I will always be with you.

Your inner child,
Cookie

Other People's Stories

At this workshop, I was amazed how open people were about telling their troubles and life stories. It surprised me that they could speak so easily about their hardships. As they spoke, most kept their emotions intact. It hurt my heart just to listen to some of their struggles, traumas, and unpleasant experiences. I am very sympathetic and empathetic. I easily cry while reading a novel or viewing a sad movie. I needed a tissue while I listened to their stories.

In this group, both women and men had lost their spouses to divorce, illness, or sudden death. They had to struggle with grief, loneliness, financial issues, and now being half of a couple. There were parents who survived their children's deaths due to miscarriage, illness, accident, or suicide. Some of the adults were molested or raped as children or teenagers. Finally, they were dealing with these deeply buried traumas.

The story that upset me the most was a mother who lost her teenager to suicide. I can't tell her story because she is putting it in her own book. But let me unload my reaction to her as she was telling it. She began by talking about the joy she experienced being pregnant and the delight of raising a beautiful little girl. Having two daughters of my own I could easily relate to that. I smiled both inwardly and outwardly while remembering my own daughters as toddlers. What a delight they were.

However, as she spoke to us, her ~~voice grew tight~~ in her throat, and her body appeared to be strained into an overly erect, controlled posture. The PT in me saw and felt her tension as she was trying to stay in control of her emotions. She looked like a glass about to drop onto a marble floor and splinter into a million fragments. As she described her daughter's preteen years when the girl was into drugs and self-mutilation, the mother's composure dropped. The speaker's thin body shivered and shook as she emitted mournful sobs between her words. Her daughter fought therapy and openly talked about suicide. She even managed to run away when she was institutionalized in a teen drug facility.

The mother spoke softly about a lovely day she shared with the daughter, which made her feel that the daughter was turning over a new leaf. It was the very next day that the mother found the girl dead in her bedroom from a drug overdose. At this point, the mother stopped talking and slowly sank back into her chair. For many minutes the room was encased in stone silence.

I, along with the other mothers in the group, was frozen in my seat with my heart pumping loudly in my chest. My eyes and nose were running uncontrollably.

I needed more tissues. The voice inside my head kept yelling at me, "This isn't a novel or a movie." This remarkable mother has organized many different fundraisers in memory of her daughter to help other troubled teenagers.

That night, I made sure to phone all my grandchildren just to hear their voices and learn about their day. I needed to tell them how much I loved them and how special they are to me. These phone connections were very grounding for me.

The question my family and I have wrestled with for years is, why was I born legally blind? Nobody knows. Mine is not a medical problem because there is no operation, exercise or medicine to correct it. The rest of my growth and development was completely normal.

To look at me or any other person in this group of writers, you would never know what troubles each of us was dealing with. As I continue to learn nearly every day, people are amazingly good at concealing their inner turmoil, pain, and issues. It is only by befriending the person that you can truly understand the struggles they are dealing with.

Many of us in this workshop were using the written word to transform ourselves from the depths of grief, pain, and suffering so that we can help others who are dealing with their own heavy baggage. I have found that by giving to others, my load becomes lighter. I feel that this is the true meaning of the Hebrew word *tzedukah* (charity).

The Trip Home

My trip home from Costa Rica provided its own problematic moments. Liberia is a small airport. Once inside, the first thing the nine of us authors needed to do was to fill out customs forms. One of my new friends read her form out loud so that we could fill in our forms simultaneously. We then went to the luggage counter to drop off our large bags. There I was given my boarding pass. Thank goodness I didn't have to fidget with a machine to get it. This same friend was going to the gate next to mine. She walked me to my gate, confirmed that it was going to Miami and that I was in the right place. She made me feel so cared for. We hugged, and she was off. I watched her slowly disappear into the crowd.

I had a preassigned seat on the plane, so I wasn't concerned about being in group seven, the last group to be called to board the aircraft. It was a full flight, so I was lucky that there still was room in the overhead compartment for my computer case, which helped me to relax.

Midway through this flight, the stewardess passed out the immigration forms. She ran out of the forms two rows before my seat. That meant that I wouldn't have to ask a stranger to help me fill it out on the plane. We were told to pick up the forms when we got off the plane in Miami. I decided not to worry in advance. I have an advanced degree in worrying, especially when I'm flying solo.

I just read my Kindle. I love the Kindle because it is lighter than most books, and I can carry many books with me and it never gets any heavier. My favorite thing about the Kindle is I can adjust the size of the print so I can read it without glasses. I hate wearing glasses in public. Even though I'm now a senior citizen, I suppose my adolescent vanity is still a part of me.

Once again, like a traveling pro, I deplaned and followed the crowd to the passport checkpoint line. No one was handing out immigration forms anywhere. I asked a young couple I was standing next to if they had their form. The woman said that she had an extra one, but it was in Spanish. Neither of us read or spoke Spanish. She gave it to me and read me the questions from her English form. We were in the middle of completing the form when she and her husband were told to move to another line. I was directed to a large room with many machines that passengers were standing in front of and pushing buttons. As I got closer, I saw these machines had the immigration forms on it to fill out.

Once again, I controlled myself from going into panic mode by standing erect and breathing slowly. I checked the machine print and realized that I couldn't read it because it was small and the background was too bright. I looked for someone in uniform. Of course, there was nobody like that in this large room. I stood in the middle of the room just turning slowly around in a circle, keeping panic at bay.

Finally, a man wearing a uniform walked in. I practically lunged at him. I told him that I had trouble seeing and couldn't use the machine. Would he please help me? I think he might have been a pilot. He was very kind and read the questions. He even offered me some humorous answers that I opted not to use. These were the same questions that were on the paper form. The machine copied my passport and then took a photo of me. I didn't look glamorous; in fact, I hardly looked presentable.

I thanked the man, and we both went on our separate ways. I gave out a big sigh of relief. My guardian angels were really with me today. They just let me sweat a little first.

I continued through another line until it was my turn to hand this piece of paper in and show my passport. No problem! I congratulated myself for overcoming another stumbling block as I walked to baggage claim. I assumed now I was home free and easy. My luggage was decorated with colorful pom-poms and large Z's, making the suitcase easy for me to find.

Herm would be waiting at the cell phone lot. I would call him as soon as I picked up my luggage and went outside. With each successful transaction behind me, my confidence and pride in myself and my ability to deal with whatever came up grew. I was certain I had just completed the final hurdle of this trip.

Not so! At baggage claim there were at least three carousels. So I asked a uniformed porter pushing a large luggage cart, where the luggage was for Flight 4480 coming from Costa Rica. The porter pointed to a large electronic board many feet away and high up near the ceiling. I kept my voice calm as I politely stated I couldn't read that board. Could he please tell me where I could find my luggage? After glancing up at the board he finally said, "Belt 3" and pointed the way with his index finger. I thanked him and walked over to where the luggage was circling on Belt 3.

After twenty minutes of watching other passengers find their suitcases, I walked around to see if mine had been removed from the belt. It wasn't in the pile of luggage standing next to this belt. I wondered aloud and finally one of the porters pointed to another pile of luggage sitting at a different carousel. I walked over and there it was. With both my breathing and heart rate back to normal, I headed for the exit clutching my Z-decorated luggage and pulling it behind me.

I again just followed the crowd down two ramps until I was at street level. I practically skipped outside and across the street to the car pick up where I phoned Herm to come get me. It took him almost half an hour. Traffic crawled, and people took time and space as they picked up their friends and family. Herm spotted me and called on the cell phone. He knows all cars look the same to me, and I can't recognize his car. He pulled in close to where I was standing. We threw my luggage in the trunk of the car and, after a quick hello kiss, off we went slowly easing into the flow of traffic.

I made it to Costa Rica and back again flying solo! I thought traveling alone would get easier with each trip. Unfortunately, that's not so. Each trip seems to have its own conundrum for me, something that I couldn't foresee. It forces me to find the right people to ask questions to get the correct information. I have to be polite when people tell me where to look to get the information I need. I really want to shout, "Idiot, if I could see to read that far away, I would not have to ask you for help!" Then I have to disclose my vision problem. I always find that difficult and embarrassing.

The good news is that I recognize when I am forced to seek help. For me, traveling alone is nerve wracking. But I have learned to put one foot in front of the other and just move on. If I don't travel alone some of the time, I will miss out on things I want and need to do, like this terrific transformational writing workshop in Costa Rica.

One of the major things I got from this workshop was how to ask for what I need and not to be overly embarrassed by talking about my visual problems when I need help. Writing this sentence makes it sound very easy and simple. Most people wouldn't have a problem. But for me it was a major hurdle to jump over. I am revealing a deep, dark secret about myself to strangers. This was a big no-no in my formative years. And, I have faithfully adhered to this dictum most of my life.

A few months after Costa Rica at another workshop closer to home, the leader asked me to write a letter to a good or dear friend and share my secret. She really wasn't sure I could do it. I, too, doubted that I had the courage to do it.

I wrote a one-page typed letter, which was extremely emotionally draining and difficult. That same night, before I lost my nerve, I shared the letter over the telephone with a dear and trusted friend. I was totally shocked and humbled by her response. She said she was honored that I shared my secret with her.

The next day, I privately read the letter to the group leader. It was still extremely difficult. There were many feelings of shame, guilt, and fear arising within me as I read. At the last minute before our workshop concluded, I read my letter to this group of transformational authors.

They had already accepted me with my bionic reading glasses, so I took the next step and read them my letter. As I read, the leader had to steady me as my body trembled. She also took my hand off the bouncing mouse as I read from my laptop. Tears blurred the large-print words on my computer screen. As I read, I gulped for air and swallowed my words with sobs. My new author friends were a kind, caring, receptive audience. When I finished, they had gentle words and hugs for me. This made me feel like I had crossed over another difficult bridge.

I wanted to share this letter with you my readers. However, it has mysteriously disappeared. There was no printed copy. It is nowhere to be found in my computer system. I believe it is floating in cyberspace. For me it was a means to an end. The more I tried to rewrite this letter, the quicker my mind shuts down on me. It was a very emotional letter. I remember crying deeply as I wrote. The words just seemed to form themselves on the page. And as the words formed, my body went through a metamorphosis of feelings and emotions: anger, frustration, fear, inadequacy, and repeatedly asking, "Why me?"

I can't believe I really wrote and read the letter. It was so out of character for me. It meant that I was growing, changing, and evolving. Wow! Why it disappeared is a mystery to be solved another day or maybe never.

Slowly, I am spreading my wings and taking flight by sharing my story. Liftoff has been accomplished by publicly acknowledging my disability and the struggles it has caused me. Landing will be personally and publicly announcing and acknowledging my accomplishments. I truly am able to fly solo. Yes, we all show our courage in different ways.

Courage

I wish that your eyes would see and your ears hear your soul's truth of who you really are. So that truth can uplift others in your presence to their own inner knowing. Say yes to whatever stretches and expands you, even if it frightens you. Courage is the necessary force ensuring growth rather than retreat.

Firemen show physical courage every time they walk into a burning building. Parents exhibit courage when they take a risk for the sake of their children. Social courage helps parents accept their children's conditions and not hide them from the public. In doing so, they bring up children who are not ashamed of their disabilities. Moral courage helps peoples say no to violence.

Through exercising courage, we make our lives and the lives of those around us better.

I have shown courage in managing my way around airports.

Action Exercise

Where and how do you manifest courage?

Dis the Dis in Disability!

I forgive myself, I accept myself, and I love myself.

Disability is a physical or mental condition that limits a person's mobility, dexterity, or stamina. It includes impairments, such as respiratory disorders, blindness, epilepsy, sleep disorders, cerebral palsy, mental retardation, depression, spinal cord injury, visual impairment, deafness, arthritis, and muscular dystrophy. Some terms used to denote a disability are: disorder, dysfunction, affliction, ailment, incapacity, special needs, learning disability, handicapped, infirmity, and disablement.

It has been noted that throughout history the disabled have usually been poorly treated. The assumption was that they were defective, unhealthy, and deviant. These disabilities often lead families to abandon them. Society treated them as objects of fear and pity. It was assumed that such individuals were incapable of participating in or contributing to society and that they must rely on welfare or charitable originations. Thus, offensive terms have frequently been used to define and label the disabled: abnormality, defective, impairment, oddity, unfitness, idiot, imbecile, moron, infirmity, and malady

During World War II, Hitler labeled the killing of the sick and disabled mercy killing. The Nazis had a euthanasia program to eliminate what they called "life unworthy of life." They gassed these individuals. They also eliminated the unfit through starvation, using them as guinea pigs for medical experiments, and objects for soldier training practice.

Many families tended to place these individuals in institutions where many suffered abuse and neglect, substandard health and safety conditions, lack of their rights, forms of electric shock therapy, painful restraints, neglect, seclusion, experimental treatments and procedures.

During the 1940s and 1950s with the returning injured and disabled soldiers of World War II, the Federal government provided them with financial compensation and vocational rehabilitation. This action caused both government-funded and charitable programs to focus on rehabilitation rather than institutionalization.

I have never thought of myself as disabled. Maybe just incapacitated in certain circumstances, that's all. Maybe that's one of the many reasons I became a physical therapist. I could help people in need to improve their physical health and with it help them have a more positive attitude toward their situation. Though at the time I was not conscious of all this. But I do see it now as I am looking back.

Just as I had idols growing up, I have decided to think of present-day people who have surmounted their problems and disabilities to be acknowledged as experts in their life endeavors. Here is a brief look at some famous people that did not let a major physical disability hold them back from success.

Blindness is defined as lacking visual perception because of neurological or physiological factors. Total blindness is the lack of seeing form or light perception.

Louis Braille, the inventor of the Braille writing system, became blind by accidentally stabbing himself in the eye with his father's awl. Braille is an organized system of small bumps which represents letters. Thus

Braille is a tactile rather than visual reading system for those who are blind. I was aware of Braille because of my visual disability. However, I was fortunate not to need his invention.

The first deaf and blind person to graduate from college was **Helen Keller**. A childhood illness caused her to be both blind and deaf. She became a famous speaker and author. She was a strong advocate for people with disabilities.

During the American Civil War, **Harriet Tubman,** an escaped slave, became an abolitionist, humanitarian, and Union spy. She was also called the conductor of the Underground Railroad. She helped many slaves escape slavery through the Underground Railroad. In reality the Underground Railroad was neither a railroad nor underground. It was called "underground" because of its secretive nature. And "railroad" because it was an emerging form of transportation. In reality, it was a secret network of safe houses, churches, and farms that offered shelter and safety to runaway slaves. The stations were secret hideouts such as passages, basements, cellars, and compartments in cupboards where slaves were safely hidden.

Tubman's blindness and seizure disorder were the result of a hard blow to the head from a heavy metal object thrown at a runaway slave but instead struck her.

I had a girlfriend who lived in one of the homes Tubman lived in. She told me all about Harriet whom I had never heard of. She also showed me cupboards in her home where slaves were hidden.

The American music magazine *Rolling Stone* named **Stevie Wonder** the ninth greatest singer of all time. He is an American singer, songwriter, multi-instrumentalist, and record producer. He has more than thirty top hits. He has won two Grammy awards and a lifetime achievement award. He was inducted into both the Rock and Roll and Songwriter's Hall of Fame. He has been blind since birth. It was assumed that he received excessive oxygen in his incubator which caused a destructive ocular disorder affecting the retina. He also had a hearing loss.

Marla Runyan was the first legally blind marathon runner. At the age of nine she developed Stargardt's Disease, a form of macular degeneration that left her legally blind. She holds five gold medals for the Paralympics. She also finished as the top American at the 2002 New York City Marathon. She became the first blind athlete to qualify for the US Olympic team in the 1,500-meter event. She holds master's degrees in communicative disorders and special education. She was a teacher at the Perkins School for the Blind. Helen Keller was a graduate of that school.

I included Marla Runyan because like me she is legally blind. I am not a runner but a walker of marathons. I feel in some way we are kindred spirits.

There is a sense of alienation and isolation that tends to come with a hearing loss. Hearing loss is usually gradual and invisible to others.

Whoopi Goldberg, actress, comic, and cohost of *The View* on ABC feels her hearing loss came from listening to loud music to close to her ears for many years. She admits to wearing hearing aids. She uses her story as an example to youngsters to keep them from abusing the volume on their listening devices.

Gerard Butler is an actor who has starred in over 300 film and stage productions. He had surgery as a child that left his right ear physically deformed. He suffers from tinnitus (ringing in the ears) and hearing loss in that ear. However, his condition didn't prevent him from staring and singing in the film version of the musical *Phantom of the Opera*.

Actress **Halle Berry** lost her hearing because of domestic abuse. This toxic relationship cost her eighty percent of her hearing in one ear. This didn't stop her from becoming one of the highest-grossing women in Hollywood. She has become a spokeswoman for domestic abuse victims.

Barbra Streisand, actress and singer, has struggled with life-long tinnitus. This ringing in the ears increases in stressful situations. In one situation it was so intense she had to walk off the stage during a performance.

Barbra lived in Brooklyn and also went to Erasmus Hall High School at the same time I was there. But we were in different grades.

Then there is the overall inclusive category of physically disabled. Here are some famous people that didn't see their disabilities as insurmountable obstacles but challenges that would push them to achieve great things.

One of my father's favorite presidents was FDR, **Franklin Delano Roosevelt**. He led our country through the Great Depression and World War II. He also strongly advocated for the disabled. He himself was in a wheelchair because polio left his lower extremities paralyzed.

Stephen Hawking was a professor of mathematics for thirty years. He directed the Center for Theoretical Cosmology and has received numerous honorary degrees. He is the author of many books. He is also known for his pioneering work in black holes and relativity.

At the age of twenty-one, he was diagnosed with ALS, also known as Lou Gehrig's Disease. He was told that he probably wouldn't live to see age twenty-five. However, at age twenty-seven he became wheelchair bound. He used a single cheek muscle attached to a speech-generating device and continued to teach and research throughout his life. He fought this disease and would not let it interfere with his career. If asked, he would say, "Live life to the fullest. Never focus on disability." He passed away on March 14, 2018 at the age of seventy-six. How is that for beating the odds?

I feel Stephen Hawking stands out as the symbol of success in spite of a very severe and life-threatening disability. I would herald him as my "poster person" for success. Now is the time to "Dis" the "Dis" in Disability!

Itzhak Perlman is an Israeli-American violinist and orchestra conductor. He began playing the violin at age three. Around that time, he became paralyzed by polio and confined to a wheelchair. The doctors didn't think that he should pursue a music career.

But he didn't listen to them and followed his dream. As a teenager, he played on the *Ed Sullivan Show*. He also played at a state dinner for Queen Elizabeth and at Barack Obama's inauguration. He is recognized as one of the world's premier violinists.

Dad told me that he played the violin in his youth. I never saw him with a violin or heard him play. Dad enjoyed listening to music and the news on the radio.

More recently there is a category called learning disabled. I have trouble believing these famous men are listed here.

Albert Einstein, mathematician, physicist, was dyslexic. In school he had difficulty with math and expressing himself.

Alexander Graham Bell, inventor of the telephone, was learning disabled. Bell is important to me because I collect telephones.

Thomas Edison, inventor of the phonograph, the electric light bulb, telegraphs, did not read until he was twelve. He had scarlet fever at age fourteen that caused his deafness.

Do you recognize any of these famous people? Who else comes to mind? I tried to pick celebrities that are well known and popular. Einstein, Edison, FDR, and Keller are people that we learn about in school. Were you aware of any of these celebrities or their disabilities? Or more importantly, their successes?

Just recently while writing this chapter, I had a severe head cold. When it abated, I totally lost my hearing. This had never happened before. I was surrounded by total silence. My left ear was painful. Both ears felt like they had a balloon in them that kept inflating. I could see people talking to me but heard absolutely nothing. Not only was this frightening, but it made me feel isolated and alone.

When I could not get an immediate appointment with an ear, nose, and throat doctor, I went to an emergency-care office. There the nurse practitioner prescribed ear drops to be used in both ears after he removed wax from my right ear.

By the time I saw an ENT doctor, I could hear very loud sounds but still had trouble hearing a conversational voice. This doctor prescribed a variety of medications and a nasal spray. I was to stop the ear drops and put nothing in my ears. The doctor told me it could take up to six weeks before my hearing returned. Six weeks seemed like forever. That was not what I wanted to hear, but at least it gave me some hope.

I have no trouble talking. However, carrying on a simple conversation was difficult. I keep asking loudly in my Brooklyn accent "Wha'd ye say?" When at the pool with a group of friends, I watched an animated conversation with lots of laughter and had no idea what they were talking about. It made me feel so separated and alone, I wanted to cry. But, I held my tears. Eventually, my hearing did return, thank goodness!

I never imagined myself writing a book, especially one that so exposed myself. But now that I have come to the last chapter, I can see how it has helped me to heal physically, psychologically, and even socially. Somehow through writing I have found my voice. I have been able to share my deep, dark, buried secret. Until now I never realized how that secret had controlled every aspect of my life. I have openly shared my life's story and shared some of the raw emotions I so tightly tucked away. It wasn't easy. There were many tears shed over the words on these pages.

Writing has helped me to sort out many of my deep emotional issues and find a framework to make sense of my life. I am finding a new direction of self-worth and positivity. I believe at this point I can reframe my life's story. With this painful experience behind me, I am moving forward with zest, showing myself how accomplished I really am.

Like all of us, people with disabilities want to be recognized for their **abilities**. So help me with my campaign to **Dis the Dis in Disability.**

Referring to people with a disability

Disability is not an illness or health problem. People with disabilities are not patients nor are they superheroes. Disability is an umbrella term covering impairments, activity limitations, and participation restrictions.

Don't assume that people with disabilities are willing to discuss their disability. Some people prefer not to be publicly identified as a person with a disability. I put myself in that category. I call it a fact of life.

Action Exercise:

Below are some concrete and socially acceptable ways to interact with a disabled person.

Here are is a list of *don'ts* when talking to a disabled person:

1. Don't talk louder to a physically disabled person. They are disabled, not deaf.
2. Ask before helping.
3. Don't lean on the wheelchair.
4. Talk directly to the person in the wheelchair, not the person with him.
5. Introduce yourself when speaking with the visually impaired.
6. Face a deaf person when speaking to him.
7. If you don't know the person, avoid remarks like, "You are so inspirational." This inadvertently implies that a person with a disability lacks or has limited skill or talents.

When writing or speaking about the disabled.

1. Don't use subjective terms such as *afflictive with, victim of, troubled with, suffering from.* Such expressions convey negative connotations. It is better to say a person who has a (specific) disability.

2. Emphasize the individual, not the disability

3. Don't compare a disability to a disease.

4. Don't refer to a person with a disability as a patient.

ACKNOWLEDGEMENTS

I especially appreciate you who are holding this book in your hands right now. If you found it beneficial, I'd love to hear from you. Contact me at zorapt@email.com. Maybe you would be kind enough to write a review.

I warmly want to thank: cousin Carolyn Starman Hessel and friends Marilyn Nathan, Mary McCann, and Carol Winkler who read the various drafts of my memoir and gave me the benefits of their writing expertise, understanding, insight, encouragement, and emotional support.

Christine Kloser, Jean Merrill, and Carrie Jareed, thanks for traveling with me from the very beginning to the end of this writing adventure.

Last but most important is my computer guru husband, Herman. I can't count how many times he came to my rescue when I had a computer mishap.

To those, who like me are, "Dis"-ing a disability, I wish you strength and courage.

ABOUT THE AUTHOR

Zora Natanblut grew up in Brooklyn during the 1940s and 50s. She met her husband at age seventeen when they were both counselors at summer camp. They have lived most of their fifty-seven years of marriage in King of Prussia, Pennsylvania. They spend the winter months in Florida enjoying the warm weather and the many wonderful activities of a senior community. Winters in Florida was a tradition established by their parents and Zora's grandparents. Her family consists of two daughters, a son, and six terrific grandchildren.

Zora graduated from Adelphia College with a BA in psychology and from Gratz College with honors with an MA in education. She received her degree in physical therapy from the University of Pennsylvania. She transitioned from a medical-model physical therapist to a holistic, hands-on physical therapist after becoming certified in CranioSacral therapy and the Alexander

Technique. She also studied and incorporated many other hands-on therapeutic techniques. She frequently taught Alexander and CranioSacral workshops.

She is an avid collector of antique telephones. Her friends have called her home a telephone museum.